THE French TRAVELMATE

Compiled by Lexus

Chronicle Books · San Francisco

Cover design: Kathy Warinner
Composition: TBH Typecast

ISBN: 0-87701-872-3

10 9 8 7 6 5 4 3 2 1

Chronicle Books
275 Fifth Street
San Francisco, California 94103

 printed on recycled paper

YOUR TRAVELMATE gives you one single A–Z list of useful words and phrases to help you communicate in French. Built into this list are travel tips, with facts and figures which provide valuable information; French words you'll see on signs and notices; and typical replies to some of the things you might want to say. There is a menu reader on pp. 82–83, and numbers are given on the last page.

Your TRAVELMATE also tells you how to pronounce French. Just read the pronunciations as though they were English, and you will communicate – although you might not sound like a native speaker. The typical French nasal sounds are represented by [o͞n] and [a͞n]. [j] is like the second consonant sound in "measure" or "seizure". Practice and listening to the French will soon help you distinguish between difficult sounds.

Depending on the likely context of use, the TRAVELMATE gives the French equivalent of either "the" or "a". In some cases, you will also find "du", "de la" or plural "des", for English "some". The feminine form of adjectives has not, as a rule, been given; remember that the final consonant is sounded in the feminine form: chaud, chaude [shoh, shohd], creux, creuse [krer, krerz], certain, certaine [sair-ta͞n, sair-ten]

The present tense of verbs will be sufficient to help you get by in most situations:
arriver [ahree-vay]–j'arrive [jah-reev], tu arrives [too ah-reev], il (elle) arrive [eel, el ah-reev], nous arrivons [nooz ahree-von], vous arrivez [vooz ahree-vay], ils (elles) arrivent [eels, elz ah-reev]

Finally, you may need to spell your name:
a [ah] b [bay] c [say] d [day] e [ay] f [eff] g [jay] h [ash] i [ee] j [jee] k [kah] l [el] m [em] n [en] o [oh] p [pay] q [koo] r [airr] s [ess] t [tay] u [oo] v [vay] w [doobler vay] x [eeks] y [ee-grek] z [zed]

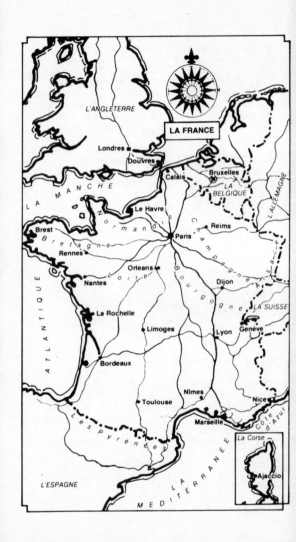

a, an un (une) [a͞n, oon]

  5 francs a liter cinq frances le litre [sa͞n fro͞n ler leetr]

aboard à bord [ah-bor]

about: about 15 environ quinze [o͞nvee-ro͞n ka͞nz]

  about 2 o'clock vers deux heures [vair . . .]

above: au-dessus (de . . .) [oh der-soo]

abroad à l'étranger [ah laytro͞n-jay]

absolutely absolument [apsoh-loo-mo͞n]

accelerator l'accélérateur [axay-lay-rah-terr]

accept accepter [axep-tay]

accrès interdit no entry

accident un accident [axee-do͞n]

  there's been an accident il y a eu un accident [eelyah oo . . .]

» *TRAVEL TIP: if anybody is hurt, get the police; for minor accidents, make sure both parties sign the "constat à l'amiable"*

accommodation: we need accommodation for 3 il nous faut de la place pour trois personnes [eel noo foh der lah plass . . .]

» *TRAVEL TIP: go to the local "syndicat d'initiative" (tourist office) for information; one- or two-star hotels are almost always a good bet; also "gîtes ruraux" (self-catering accommodation) and "gîtes d'étape" (dormitory accommodations for hikers, etc.)*

accotements non stabilisés soft shoulder

accountant un comptable [ko͞n-tahbl]

accurate précis

A.C.F. = *Automobile Club de France, like AAA*

ache: it aches c'est douloureux [say dooloo-rer]

....

my back aches j'ai mal au dos [jay
maloh-doh]
across: across (the river) de l'autre côté (de la
rivière) [der loht koh-tay der . . .]
  to get across traverser [trahvair-say]
adaptor un adaptateur [ahdap-tah-terr]
add ajouter [ahjoo-tay]
address une adresse [ah-dress]
  will you give me your address? est-ce que
vous pouvez me donner votre adresse? [esker
voo poovay mer doh-nay . . .]
adhesive bandage un pansement adhésif
[pōns-mōn ahday-zeef]
adjust ajuster [ahjoos-tay]
admission *(to disco, etc.)* l'entrée [ōn-tray]
advance: can we reserve in advance? est-ce
qu'on peut réserver à l'avance? [eskōn per
rayzair-vay ah lah-vōns]
advertisement une annonce [ah-nōns]
afraid: I'm afraid I don't know je regrette, je
ne sais pas [jer rer-gret . . .]
  he's afraid of . . . il a peur de . . . [eel ah per
der]
after après [ah-pray]
  after you après vous
afternoon l'après-midi [ahpray-mee-dee]
  in the afternoon l'après-midi
aftershave un aftershave
again de nouveau [noo-voh]
against contre [kōntr]
age l'âge [ahj]
  under age mineur [mee-nerr]
  ages très longtemps [tray lōn-tōn]
agent un représentant [rerpray-sōn-tōn]
ago: a week ago il y a une semaine [eelyah . . .]
  it wasn't long ago il n'y a pas longtemps
[eelnyah-pah . . .]
  how long ago? il y a combien de temps?
[kōnb-yān . . .]
agree: I agree je suis d'accord [jer swee dah-kor]

it doesn't agree with me ça ne me convient pas [san mer kōnv-yān pah]

air l'air

by air en avion [ānn ahv-yōn]

by airmail par avion

with air-conditioning climatisé [kleemah-tee-zay]

airport l'aéroport [ah-ayroh-por]

alarm: give the alarm donnez l'alarme

alarm clock un réveil [ray-vay]

alcohol l'alcool [al-kol]

is it alcoholic? est-ce que c'est alcoolisé? [. . . alkolee-zay]

alimentation food

alive vivant [vee-vōn]

is he still alive? est-ce qu'il vit encore?

all *(everything)* tout [too]

(everybody) tous (toutes) [toos, toot]

it's all right, I'm all right ça va [sah vah]

all right! d'accord! [dah-kor]

that's all c'est tout [say-too]

thank you, not at all merci, de rien [mairsee der ree-yān]

all night toute la nuit, **all day** toute la journée

all I have/want tout ce que j'ai/je veux [toos-ker . . .]

allergic: I'm allergic to . . . je suis allergique à . . . [jer swee ahlair-jeek]

allowed: is it allowed? est-ce que c'est permis? [eskersay pair-mee]

allow me . . . permettez-moi . . .

allumez vos phares headlights on

almost presque [presk]

alone seul [serl]

did you come here alone? est-ce que vous êtes venu ici tout seul? [esker voo zait ver-noo . . .]

leave me alone! laissez-moi tranquille! [lay-say mwah trōn-keel]

already déjà [day-jah]

....

also aussi [oh-see]
although bien que [bee-yān ker]
altogether ensemble [ōn-sonbl]
  what does that make altogether? qu'est-ce
  que ça fait au total? [kesker sah fay oh toh-tal]
always toujours [too-joor]
a.m.: 10 a.m. dix heures du matin [. . . doo
  mah-tān]
ambassador l'ambassadeur [ōnbah-sah-derr]
ambulance l'ambulance [ōnboo-lōns]
  get an ambulance! appelez une ambulance!
» *TRAVEL TIP: no 911; in an emergency call "Police
  Secours"*
America l'amérique [ahmay-rik]
  American américain [ahmay-ree-kān]
among parmi [. . . mee]
amp ampère [ōn-pair]
  15 amp fuse un fusible de 15 ampères
  [foo-zeebl . . .]
anchor l'ancre [ōnkr]
and et [ay]
angry fâché [fah-shay]
  don't get angry ne vous fâchez pas [ner voo
  fah-shay pah]
ankle la cheville [sher-vee]
anniversary: it's our anniversary c'est notre
  anniversaire de mariage [ahnee-vair-sair der
  mahr-yahj]
annoy: he's annoying me il m'importune
  [ānpor-toon]
  it's very annoying c'est très ennuyeux
  [ōn-nwee-yer]
another: can we have another room? est-ce
  qu'on peut avoir une autre chambre? [eskōn
  per ah-vwahr oon-ohtr . . .]
  another beer, please encore une bière, s'il
  vous plaît
answer une réponse [ray-pōns]
  to answer répondre
  there's no answer on ne répond pas
antifreeze l'antigel [ōntee-jel]

any: have you got any bread/water? est-ce que
vous avez du pain/de l'eau? [. . . doo pan, der
loh]

have you got any rooms? est-ce que vous
avez des chambres? [. . . day shonbr]

we haven't got any money/tickets nous
n'avons pas d'argent/de billets [. . . dahr-jon,
der bee-yay]

I haven't got any je n'en ai pas [jer nonn ay
pah]

anybody: is anybody there? est-ce qu'il y a
quelqu'un? [eskeel yah kel-kan]

we don't know anybody here nous ne
connaissons personne ici [. . . pair-son]

anything: have you got anything for . . . est-ce
que vous avez quelque chose pour . . .
[. . . kelker-shoz . . .]

I don't want anything je n'ai besoin de rien
[. . . ree-yan]

apartment un appartement [ahpahr-ter-mon]

aperitif un apéritif

apology des excuses [ex-kooz]

please accept my apologies je vous prie de
m'excuser [jer voo pree der mexkoo-zay]

appellation contrôlée *quality label: a guarantee
that a wine comes from one particular area*

appendicitis l'appendicite [ahpan-dee-seet]

appetite: I've lost my appetite j'ai perdu
l'appétit [. . . ahpay-tee]

apple une pomme

application form un formulaire d'inscription
[formoo-lair danskrips-yon]

appointment un rendez-vous

can we make an appointment? est-ce que
nous pouvons prendre rendez-vous? [esker noo
poovon prondr ronday-voo]

appuyer *push*

apricot un abricot [ahbree-koh]

April: in April en avril [an nah-vreel]

area la région [rayj-yon]

in the area dans les environs [. . . onvee-ron]

....

arm le bras [brah]
around: is he around? est-ce qu'il est là?
[eskee-lay lah]
arrange: will you arrange it? est-ce que vous
pouvez vous en occuper? [esker voo poovay voo
zann-ohkoo-pay]
  it's all arranged tout est réglé
arrest arrêter [ahray-tay]
arrêt stop
arrival l'arrivée
arrive arriver [ahree-vay]
  we only arrived yesterday nous ne sommes
arrivés qu'hier
art l'art [ahr]
art gallery un musée [moo-zay]
arthritis: he has arthritis il a de l'arthrite
[. . . der lar-treet]
artificial artificiel [ahrtee-fees-yel]
artist un artiste [ahr-teest]
as: as big/quickly as possible aussi [ohsee]
grand/rapidement que possible
  as much/many as you can autant [oh-tōn]
que vous pouvez
  do as I do faites comme moi [fait kom mwah]
  as you like comme vous voulez [kom voo
voolay]
ascenseur elevator
ashore à terre [ah tair]
ashtray un cendrier [sōndree-yay]
ask demander [dermōn-day]
  I didn't ask for that ce n'est pas ce que j'ai
demandé [ser nay pah ser ker jay . . .]
  could you ask him to . . . est-ce que vous
pouvez lui demander de . . . [esker voo
poovay . . .]
asleep: he's (still) asleep il dort [dor] (encore)
asparagus des asperges [ass-pairj]
aspirin une aspirine [aspee-reen]
asthma: she has asthma elle a de l'asthme
[. . . der lassm]
at: at the cafe au [oh] café

at my hotel à mon hôtel [ah . . .]

at one o'clock à une heure

atmosphere l'atmosphère [atmoss-fair]

attractive: I think you are very attractive
(to woman) je vous trouve très jolie
[. . . joh-lee]

it's an attractive offer c'est une offre
avantageuse [. . . ahvōn-tah-jerz]

August: in August en août [ōnn-oot]

aunt: my aunt ma tante [tōnt]

Australia l'australie [ostrah-lee]

Australian australien [ohstrahl-yān]

authorities les autorités [ohtoh-ree-tay]

automatic automatique

autumn: in the autumn en automne
[ōnn-ohton]

away: is it far away from here? est-ce que c'est
loin d'ici? [esker-say lwān dee-see]

go away! allez-vous en! [ahlay voo zōn]

awful affreux [ah-frer]

axle l'essieu [ayss-yer]

baby un bébé

we'd like a baby-sitter nous cherchons
quelqu'un pour garder les enfants [noo
shair-shōn kel-kān poor gahr-day layz ōn-fōn]

back *(part of body)* le dos [doh]

I've got a bad back je souffre des reins [jer
soofr day rān]

I'll be back soon je reviens dans un moment
[jer rerv-yān . . .]

can I have my money back est-ce que vous
pouvez me rendre mon argent? [esker voo
poovay mer rōndr . . .]

come back! revenez! [rerver-nay]

is he back? est-ce qu'il est de retour? [. . . der
rer-toor]

I go back tomorrow je rentre demain [jer
rōntr der-mān]

at the back derrière [dair-yair]

backpack un sac à dos [sak ah doh]

bacon le bacon

....

bacon and eggs du bacon avec des oeufs sur le plat [. . . ahvek day zer soor ler plah]
bad mauvais [moh-vay]
  not bad pas mal [pah mal]
  too bad! tant pis! [tōn pee]
  the milk is bad le lait a tourné [. . . ah toor-nay]
  this meat is bad cette viande n'est plus bonne [. . . ploo bōn]
bag un sac
  (handbag) un sac à main [sak ah mān]
baggage les bagages [bah-gahj]
baignade interdite no bathing
bakery une boulangerie [boolōnj-ree]
balcony balcon [bal-kōn]
ball *(soccer, etc.)* un ballon [bah-lōn]
  (tennis, golf) une balle [bahl]
ballpoint pen un stylo à bille [steeloh ah bee]
banana une banane [bah-nan]
band *(musical)* un orchestre [or-kestr]
bandage: could you change the bandage? est-ce que vous pouvez changer le bandage? [esker voo poovay shōnjay ler bōn-dahj]
bank *(establishment)* une banque [bōnk]
  (of river) la rive [reev]
» *TRAVEL TIP: opening hours 9-12 and 2-4; closed Sat. (large towns) or Mon.; early closing (noon) before a bank holiday and if bank holiday falls on Thurs. may be closed on Fri. as well; transactions carried out at one desk and money collected at another: "la caisse"*
  bank holiday un jour férié [joor fair-yay]
  see **public holidays**
bar un bar
  a bar of chocolate une tablette de chocolat [tah-blet der shohkoh-lah]
barbershop le coiffeur [kwah-ferr]
bargain: it's a real bargain c'est une bonne affaire [sayt oon bon ah-fair]
bartender le barman [bahr-man]
basket un panier [pan-yay]

bassinet un porte-bébé [pohrt-baybay]
bath un bain [bān]; *(tub)* une baignoire
[bay-nwahr]
  can I have a bath? est-ce que je peux prendre
un bain? [esker jer per prōndr in bān]
  bath towel une serviette de bain
[sairv-yet . . .]
bathing suit un maillot de bain [may-yoh . . .]
bathrobe la robe de chambre [. . . shōnbr]
bathroom la salle de bain [sahl der bān]
  we want a room with private bathroom
nous voulons une chambre avec salle de bain
[noo voo-lōn oon shōnbr . . .]
  where are the toilets? où sont les toiletts?
see also **toilet**
battery une pile [peel]
  (in car) la batterie [bat-ree]
be être [aitr]
  I am je suis [jer swee]
  you are vous êtes [voo zait]
  he/she is il/elle est [eelay, ellay]
  it's c'est [say]
  we are nous sommes [noo som]
  they are ils/elles sont [eel sōn]
  he's been ill il a été malade [eel ah ay-tay . . .]
  don't be late ne soyez pas en retard [ner
swah-yay pah zan rer-tar]
  I am cold/hungry j'ai froid/faim [jay frwah,
fān]
beach une plage [plahj]
  on the beach à la plage
» *TRAVEL TIP: topless bathing on most beaches;
pay attention to safety warnings: red flag
— no swimming; orange flag—unsafe, but
lifeguard in attendance; green flag—swimming
safe*
beans des haricots [ahree-koh]
  green beans des haricots verts [. . . vair]
  baked beans *not available as such*
beautiful beau (belle) [boh, bel]
because parce que [pahrser-ker]

because of the weather à cause du temps [ah kohz . . .]

bed un lit [lee]

I am going to bed at 10 je vais me coucher à dix heures [jer vay mer kooshay ah . . .]

you haven't made/changed my bed vous n'avez pas fait mon lit/changé les draps [voo nahvay pah fay mōn lee, shōn-jay lay drah]

bed and breakfast *(terms)* la chambre et le petit déjeuner [lah shōnbr ay ler pertee dayjer-nay]

» *TRAVEL TIP: used to be nonexistent as such in France, where there are so many inexpensive hotels; ask the local "syndicat d'initiative" about the possibility of "chambres chez l'habitant"*

bedroom une chambre [shōnbr]

bee une abeille [ah-bay]

beef du boeuf [berf]

beer de la bière [bee-yair]

draft beer bière pression [. . . prays-yōn]

» *TRAVEL TIP: for the equivalent of a half-pint of draft beer ask for "un demi pression"; the standard measure is 330 cl (½ pint = 270 cl); if you simply ask for "une bière" you may be served bottled beer (more expensive); if you ask for "une bière" you will automatically be served "une bière blonde", which is lager-type beer (although it may taste different from what you are used to)*

before avant [ah-vōn]

before I leave avant de partir

I haven't been here before c'est la première fois que je viens ici [say lah prerm-yair fwah ker jerv-yān ee-see]

begin commencer [kohmōn-say]

beginner: I'm a beginner je débute [jer day-boot]

beginner's slope *(skiing)* une piste pour débutants [peest poor dayboo-tōn]

behind derrière [dair-yair]

Belgian belge [belj]

  Belgium la Belgique [bel-jeek]

believe croire [krwahr]

  I don't believe you je ne vous crois [krwah] pas

bell une cloche [klosh]

  (at door) la sonnette [soh-net]

belong: that belongs to me c'est à moi [sayt ah mwah]

  whom does this belong to? à qui est ceci? [ah kee]

below au-dessous (de . . .) [oh der-soo]

belt une ceinture [sān-toor]

bend *(in road)* un virage [vee-rahj]

berries des baies [bay]

berth *(on ship)* une couchette [koo-shet]

beside à côté de [ah koh-tay der]

best: the best . . . le meilleur . . . [may-yerr]

  it's the best vacation I've ever had ce sont les meilleures vacances de ma vie

better meilleur [may-yerr]

  haven't you got anything better? est-ce que vous n'avez rien de mieux? [. . . ree-yān der myer]

  are you feeling better? est-ce que vous vous sentez mieux? [esker voo voo sōntay myer]

  I'm feeling a lot better je me sens beaucoup mieux

between entre [ōntr]

beyond plus loin que [ploo lwān ker]

bicycle une bicyclette [bee-see . . .]

bière (à la) pression draft beer

big grand [grōn]

  a big one un grand

  have you got a bigger one? est-ce que vous en avez un plus grand? [esker voo zōnn ahvay ān ploo grōn]

bikini un bikini

bill l'addition [ahdees-yōn]

could I have the bill, please? vous me donnez l'addition, s'il vous plaît [voom doh-nay ...]

billets tickets

bindings *(ski)* les fixations [feexahs-yōn]

bird un oiseau [wah-zoh]

birthday: it's my birthday c'est mon anniversaire [ahnee-vair-sair]

  happy birthday! joyeux anniversaire! [jwah-yerz ...]

bit: just a little bit un petit morceau

  that's a bit too expensive/far c'est un peu trop cher/loin [ān-per troh ...]

bite: insect bites les piqûres d'insectes [pee-koor dān-sekt]

  I've been bitten *(insects)* j'ai été piqué [jay ay-tay pee-kay]

  I've been bitten by a dog j'ai été mordu par un chien [jay aytay mordoo par ān shee-yān]

bitter amer [ah-mair]

black noir [nwahr]

  he's had a blackout il a eu une syncope [sān-kop]

blanket une couverture [koovair-toor]

bleach de l'eau de javel [ohd jah-vel]

bleed saigner [sayn-yay]

  he's bleeding il saigne [sayn]

bless you! *(after sneeze)* à vos souhaits! [ah voh sway]

blind aveugle [ah-vergl]

  his lights were blinding me ses phares méblouissaient [... maybloo-ee-say]

  blind spot l'angle mort [lōngl-mor]

blister une ampoule [ōnpool]

blocked *(pipe, etc.)* bouché [boo-shay]

  (road, etc.) barré [bah-ray]

blonde une blonde [blōnd]

blood le sang [sōn]

  blood test une prise de sang [preez der sōn]

  his blood type is ... son groupe sanguin est ... [sōn groop sōn-ghān ay]

I've got high blood pressure j'ai de la tension [jayd lah tōns-yōn]

he needs a blood transfusion il faut lui faire une transfusion [trōns-fooz-yōn] de sang

blouse un chemisier [shermeez-yay]

blue bleu [bler]

board: full board la pension complète [pōns-yōn kōn-plet]

half board la demi-pension

boarding pass la carte d'embarquement [. . . dōnbar-ker-mōn]

boat un bateau [bah-toh]

body le corps [kor]

bodywork la carrosserie [kahross-ree]

boil *(on skin)* un furoncle [foo-rōnkl]

(verb) bouillir [boo-yeer]

it's boiling ça bout [sah boo]

do we have to boil the water? est-ce qu'il faut faire bouillir l'eau? [eskeel foh fair . . .]

boiled egg un oeuf à la coque [ānn erf ah lah kok]

bone un os [oss]

(in fish) une arête [ah-ret]

book *(noun)* un livre [leevr]

bookstore une librairie [leebray-ree]

boot *(shoe)* une chaussure [shoh-soor]

rubber boots des bottes de caoutchouc [bot der kahoo-tshoo]

border la frontière [frōnt-yair]

bored: I'm bored je m'ennuie [jer mōn-nwee]

boring ennuyeux [ōn-nwee-yer]

born: I was born in je suis né en [jer swee nay ōn]

borrow: can I borrow . . . ? est-ce que je peux emprunter . . . ? [esker jer per ōnprān-tay]

boss le chef [shef]

both les deux [lay der]

I'll take both of them je prends les deux

bottle une bouteille [boo-tey]

(for baby) un biberon [beeb-rōn]

bottle opener un ouvre-bouteille [oovr-boo-tey]

bottom: at the bottom of the hill au pied de la colline [oh pyay der lah koh-leen]

bowels les intestins [āntes-tāṅ]

bowl une coupe [koop]

box une boîte [bwaht]; *(in theater)* une loge [lohj]

boy un garçon [gar-soṅ]

boyfriend: my boyfriend mon ami [ah-mee]

bra un soutien-gorge [soot-yāṅ-gorj]

bracelet un bracelet [brahs-lay]

brake *(verb)* freiner [fray-nay]

  can you check the brakes? est-ce que vous pouvez vérifier les freins? [. . . lay-frāṅ]

  I had to brake suddenly j'ai dû freiner tout à coup [jay doo fray-nay too tah koo]

  he didn't brake il n'a pas freiné

brandy le cognac [kohn-yak]

bread du pain [pāṅ]

  a loaf of bread un pain

  sliced bread du pain en tranches [trōṅsh]

  whole wheat bread du pain entier [ōṅt-yay]

  could we have some bread and butter? est-ce que vous pouvez nous apporter du pain avec du beurre? [. . . doo pāṅ ahvek doo berr]

» *TRAVEL TIP: French bread is an entirely new experience after the sliced loaf; ask for "une baguette" [oon bah-ghet] (best eaten the same day)*

break casser [kah-say]

  I think I've broken my leg/arm je crois que je me suis cassé la jambe/le bras [. . . jer mer swee kahsay lah jonb, ler brah]

  the car broke down la voiture est tombée en panne [lah vwahtoor ay tōṅ-bay ōṅ pan]

breakable fragile [frah-jeel]

breakdown *(of car)* une panne [pan]

  (nervous) une dépression nerveuse [daypress-yōṅ nair-verz]

breakfast le petit déjeuner [pertee dayjer-nay]

full breakfast un petit déjeuner à l'anglaise [. . . ah lōnglayz]

» *TRAVEL TIP: the French don't have a cooked breakfast; usually coffee with bread and butter or croissants; if you insist on a full breakfast, be prepared to pay more*

breast le sein [sān]

breath: he's getting very short of breath il a de la peine à respirer [eelah der lah pen ah respee-ray]

　breathe respirer [respee-ray]

　I can't breathe j'ai de la peine à respirer

bridge un pont [pōn]

　(game) le bridge

briefcase une serviette [sairv-yet]

brilliant brillant [bree-yōn]

bring approter [ahpor-tay]

　bring the suitcase to my hotel apportez la valise à mon hôtel

Britain la Grande-Bretagne [grōnd-brer-tan]

　British britannique [breetah-neek]

Brittany la Bretagne [brer-tan]

brochure un prospectus [prospek-toos]

　have you got any brochures about . . . ? est-ce que vous avez des prospectus sur . . . ?

broken: it's broken c'est cassé [say kah-say]

　my room/car has been broken into quelqu'un s'est introduit [say tān-troh-dwee] dans ma chambre/voiture

brooch une broche [brosh]

brother: my brother mon frère [frair]

brown brun (brune) [brān, broon]

　brown paper du papier d'emballage [pahp-yay dōnbah-lahj]

browse: can I just browse around? est-ce que je peux regarder? [esker jer per rergahr-day]

bruise une contusion [kōntooz-yōn]

brunette une brune [broon]

brush une brosse [bross]

　(painter's) un pinceau [pān-soh]

Brussels sprouts des choux de Bruxelles [shoo
   der broo-sel]
bucket un seau [soh]
buffet un buffet [boo-fay]
building un bâtiment [bahtee-mōn]
   (residential) un immeuble [ee-merbl]
bump: he bumped his head il s'est tapé la
   tête [eel say tah-pay lah tet]
bumper le pare-chocs [par-shock]
bunk une couchette [koo-shet]
   bunk beds des lits superposés [lee
   soopair-poh-zay]
buoy une bouée [boo-ay]
burglar un cambrioleur [kōnbree-oh-lerr]
   our apartment's been burglarized on a
   cambriolé [kōnbree-oh-lay] notre appartement
**burn: can you give me something for
   burns?** est-ce que vous avez quelque chose
   pour les brûlures? [esker voo zah-vay kelker-
   shohz poor lay broo-loor]
   this meat is burned cette viande est brûlée
   [broo-lay]
   my arms are burned j'ai un coup de soleil
   aux bras [jay ān koo der soh-lay . . .]
bus l'autobus [otoh-booss]
   by bus en autobus
   bus stop l'arrêt d'autobus [ahray . . .]
   bus station la gare routière [gahr root-yair]
   bus tour une excursion en autocar
   [exkoors-yōn . . .]
   could you tell me when we get there? est-ce
   que vous pouvez m'avertir quand on y arrive?
   [esker voo poovay mahvair-teer kān tōn nee
   ah-reev]
» *TRAVEL TIP: pay-as-you-enter in most cities; you
   can buy a "carnet de tickets" (book of tickets)
   from a newsstand; you must punch your ticket
   when boarding the bus and use 2 tickets if you
   are traveling further than two fare stages as
   shown on the bus route chart; "billets*

*touristiques" available for bus and subway
services*
business les affaires [ah-fair]
  (firm) une entreprise [ōntrer-preez]
  I'm here on business je suis ici pour affaires
  [jer swee zeesee . . .]
    business trip un voyage [voh-yahj] d'affaires
    it's none of your business cela ne vous
    regarde pas [ser-lah ner voo rer-gard pah]
bust la poitrine [pwah-treen]
» *TRAVEL TIP: bust measurements*

US	32	34	36	38	40
France	80	87	91	97	102

busy occupé [ohkoo-pay]
  are you busy? est-ce que vous êtes occupé?
but mais [may]
butcher une boucherie [boosh-ree]
butter du beurre [berr]
button un bouton [boo-tōn]
buy acheter [ash-tay]
  I'll buy it je l'achète [jer lah-shet]
by: I'm here by myself je suis venu seul [jer
  swee vernoo serl]
  are you here by yourself? est-ce que vous
  êtes venu seul?
  can you do it by tomorrow? est-ce que vous
  pouvez le faire d'ici à demain? [. . . dee-see ah
  der-mān]
  by train/car/plane en [ōn] train/voiture/avion
  by the church près de l'église [pray der . . .]
  who's it made by? c'est fabriqué par qui?
cabaret un spectacle [spek-tahkl] de variétés
cabbage un chou [shoo]
cabin *(on ship)* une cabine [kah-been]
cable un câble [kahbl]
cable car un téléphérique [taylay-fay-reek]
cafe un restaurant-snack
» *TRAVEL TIP: the equivalent of a truck stop is
  called "relais routier", where good and
  relatively inexpensive meals can be had*

....

café *the usual place for a drink; waiter service,*
children usually welcome; drinks cheaper at
the bar; snacks or set lunch usually available;
you can telephone from a café and there is often
a special counter where stamps and tobacco are
sold—look for a red diamond shaped TABAC
sign outside; you generally pay for your drinks
on leaving

cake un gâteau [gah-toh]
  (small) un petit gâteau

caisse cash register

calculator un calculateur [kalkoo-lah-terr]

call: will you call the manager est-ce que vous
  pouvez appeler le gérant [. . . ap-lay ler jay-rōn]
  what is this called? comment ça s'appelle?
  [komōn sah sah-pel]

calm calme
  calm down! calmez-vous! [kalmay-voo]

camera un appareil-photo [appah-rey . . .]

camp: where can we camp? où est-ce qu'on
  peut camper? [weskōn per kōn-pay]
  can we camp here? est-ce qu'on peut camper
  ici?
  we are on a camping trip nous faisons
  [fer-zōn] du camping

campsite un terrain [tay-rān] de camping

» *TRAVEL TIP: enquire at the local "syndicat*
  d'initiative" (tourist office) about location, rates
  and facilities; you may have to leave your
  passport at the campsite reception desk;
  International Camping Carnet not essential,
  but it may help or entitle you to a discount

can¹ une boîte [bwaht]
  a can of beer une bière en boîte
  (NB: bottled beer is the rule)
  can-opener un ouvre-boîte [oovr-bwaht]

can²: can I have . . . ? est-ce que je peux
  avoir . . . ? [esker jer per ah-vwahr]
  can you show me . . . ? est-ce que vous pouvez
  me montrer . . . ?

I can't swim je ne sais pas nager [jer ner say pah]

he can't... il ne peut pas...

we can't... nous ne pouvons [poo-vōn] pas...

Canada le Canada [kahnah-dah]

Canadian canadien [kahnahd-yān]

cancel: I want to cancel my reservation je veux annuler ma réservation [jer ver ahnoo-lay mah rayzair-vahs-yōn]

can we cancel dinner for tonight? est-ce que nous pouvons décommander le dîner ce soir? [... day-koh-mōn day ler dee-nay...]

candle une bougie [boo-jee]

cane une canne [kan]

capsize chavirer [shahvee-ray]

car une voiture [vwah-toor]

car keys les clés de la voiture [klay...]

by car en voiture

carafe une carafe [kah-raf]

carbonated mousseux [moo-ser]

carburetor le carburateur [karboo-rah-terr]

card une carte

do you play cards? est-ce que vous jouez aux cartes? [esker voo jway oh kart]

care: will you take care of this for me? est-ce que vous pouvez vous en occuper? [... voo-zōn noh-koo-pay]

good-bye, take care au revoir [oh rer-vwahr]

careful: be careful soyez prudent [swah-yay-proo-dōn]

car-ferry un ferry

carnation un oeillet [er-yay]

carpet un tapis [tah-pee]

carrots des carottes [kah-rot]

carry porter [por-tay]

will you carry this for me? est-ce que vous pouvez me porter ça? [esker voo poovay mer pohr-tay sah]

cartridge une cartouche [kahr-toosh]

carving une sculpture [skoolp-toor]

case *(suitcase)* une valise [vah-leez]

cash: I haven't any cash je n'ai pas d'argent liquide [jer nay pah dahr-jōn-lee-keed]
   will you cash a check for me? est-ce que vous pouvez me payer [pay-yay] un chèque?
   I'll pay cash je paye comptant [jer pay kōn-tōn]
   cash register la caisse [kes]
casino un casino [kahzee-no]
casse-croûte snack(s)
cassette une cassette [kah-set]
castle un château [shah-toh]
» *TRAVEL TIP: most castles and museums are closed on Tuesdays in France*
cat un chat [shah]
catch attraper [ahtrah-pay]
   where do we catch the bus? où est-ce qu'on prend l'autobus? [weskōn-prōn-lohtoh-boos]
   he's caught a bug il a attrapé un virus [vee-roos]
cathedral la cathédrale [kahtay-drahl]
catholic catholique [kahtoh-leek]
cauliflower un chou-fleur [shoo-flerr]
cave une grotte [grot]
ceiling le plafond [plah-fōn]
celery du céleri en branche [sail-ree ōn brōnsh]
» *TRAVEL TIP: if you see "céleri" on the menu, it will probably be "celeriac"; "céleri rémoulade" is a celeriac salad eaten as a first course*
centigrade centigrade [sōntee-grad]
» *TRAVEL TIP: to convert C to F:* $\frac{C}{5} \times 9 + 32 = F$
   centigrade −5   0 10 15 21 30 36.9
   Fahrenheit 23 32 50 59 70 86 98.4
centimeter un centimètre [sōntee-maitr]
» *TRAVEL TIP: 1 cm = 0.39 inches*
central central [sōn-trahl]
   with central heating avec le chauffage [shoh-fahj] central
center le centre [sōntr]
centre-ville city center, town center

cereal: *name the one you want: "les Corn Flakes"*
   is the best known
certain certain (certaine) [sair-tān, -ten]
   are you certain? est-ce que vous en êtes sûr?
   [esker voo zōn nait soor]
certificate un certificat [sairtee-fee-kah]
chain une chaîne [shairn]
chair une chaise [shairz]
   (easy chair) un fauteuil [foh-ter]
chairlift un télésiège [taylays-yej]
chambres rooms to let
champagne du champagne [shōn-pan]
change changer [shōn-jay]
   where can I change some money? où est-ce
   que je peux changer de l'argent? [wesker jer
   per shōn-jay der lahr-jōn]
   could you change this into francs? est-ce
   que vous pouvez me changer ça en francs?
   [. . . mer shōn-jay sah ōn frōn]
   I don't have any change je n'ai pas de
   monnaie [jer nay pah der moh-nay]
   do you have change for 10 francs? est-ce
   que vous avez la monnaie de dix francs?
   small change de la petite monnaie
   do we have to change trains? est-ce qu'il
   faut changer? [eskeel foh . . .]
   where can I get changed? où est-ce que je
   peux me changer?
Channel: the Channel la Manche [monsh]
Channel Islands les îles anglo-normandes [eel
   ōn-gloh nor-mōnd]
chantier road work ahead
charge: what will you charge? combien est-ce
   que ça va coûter? [kōnb-yān esker sah vah
   koo-tay]
   who's in charge? qui est le responsable
   [respōnsahbl] ici?
chart *(map)* une carte maritime
   [. . . mahree-teem]
chaud hot
chaussée verglacée icy road surface

cheap bon marché [bōn mahr-shay]
   is there anything cheaper? est-ce qu'il y a
   quelque chose de meilleur marché?
   [...may-yer mahr-shay]
cheat: I've been cheated je me suis fait avoir
   [jer mer swee fay ah-vwahr]
check un chèque [shek]
   checkbook le carnet de chèques
   traveler's check un traveller's cheque
   will you check? est-ce que vous pouvez
   vérifier [...vayreef-yay]
   I'm sure, I've checked j'en suis sûr, j'ai
   vérifié
   we checked in/we checked out at 10 nous
   sommes arrivés/partis à dix heures
cheek *(part of face)* la joue [joo]
cheers! *(toast)* santé! [sōn-tay]
cheese du fromage [froh-mahj]
   mild/strong cheese du fromage doux/fort
   [...doo, for]
» TRAVEL TIP: *cheese is always served before
   dessert; don't ask for crackers, as bread is
   usually eaten with cheese; there is a
   bewildering variety of cheeses: ask to sample
   before buying*
chef le chef cuisinier [...kweezeen-yay]
chess les échecs [ay-sheck]
chest la poitrine [pwah-treen]
» TRAVEL TIP: *chest measurements ("tour de
   poitrine")*

US	34	36	38	40	42	44	46
France	87	91	97	102	107	112	117

cherries des cerises [ser-reez]
chewing gum du chewing-gum [shween-gom]
chicken du poulet [poo-lay]
chickenpox la varicelle [vahree-sel]
child un enfant [ōn-fōn]
   my children mes enfants
   children's portions des portions [pors-yōn]
   pour enfants

» *TRAVEL TIP: children are generally welcome in restaurants and cafés*

chin le menton [mōn-tōn]

china la porcelaine [por-ser-lain]

chips *(at casino)* des plaques [plak]

chocolate du chocolat [shohkoh-lah]

   a box of chocolates une boîte [bwaht] de chocolats

   hot chocolate un chocolat chaud [. . . shoh]

   milk chocolate du chocolat au lait [. . . oh-lay]

   plain chocolate du chocolat à croquer [. . . ah kroh-kay]

choke *(car)* le starter (star-tair)

chop: a pork chop une côtelette de porc [koht-let der por]

Christmas: at Christmas à Noël [noh-el]

   on Christmas Eve la veille [vey] de Noël

   Merry Christmas joyeux [jwah-yer] Noël

» *TRAVEL TIP: Christmas Eve is usually an occasion for a big meal with the family or friends, "le réveillon"* [rayvay-yōn]

church une église [ay-gleez]

» *TRAVEL TIP: France being largely a Catholic country there are few Protestant churches; ask for "le temple"* [tōnpl]

chutes de pierres *falling rocks*

cider du cidre [seedr]

cigar un cigare [see-gar]

cigarette une cigarette [seegah-ret]

   would you like a cigarette? est-ce que je peux vous offrir une cigarette? [esker jer per voo zoh-freer . . .]

   filter filtre

   plain sans filtre [sōn feeltr]

circle un cercle [sairkl]

circuit touristique *scenic route*

city une ville [veel]

   city center le centre-ville [sōntrer-veel]

claim *(insurance)* une demande d'indemnité [der-mānd dāndem-nee-tay]

claret du bordeaux rouge [bor-doh rooj]
clarify clarifier [klahreef-yay]
class: 1st class, 2nd class première classe,
    deuxième classe [prerm-yair klas, derz-yem ...]
clean *(adjective)* propre [prohpr]
    can I have some clean sheets? est-ce que je
    peux avoir des draps [drah] propres?
    my room hasn't been cleaned today on n'a
    pas nettoyé ma chambre aujourd'hui
    it's not clean ce n'est pas propre
clear: I'm not clear about it je n'ai pas bien
    compris
    is the road clear? est-ce que la route est
    dégagée? [... daygah-jay]
    clear up: will it clear up later? est-ce que ça
    va s'éclaircir plus tard? [... sayklair-seer ...]
clever intelligent (intelligente) [antay-lee-jon]
climate le climat [klee-mah]
climb: we're going to climb ... nous allons
    escalader ... [eskah-lah-day]
    climber un alpiniste [alpee-neest]
    climbing boots des chaussures d'escalade
    [shoh-soor deskah-lad]
» *TRAVEL TIP: beware of rapidly changing weather*
    conditions; let somebody know where you plan
    to go; ask the local C.A.F. (Club Alpin
    Français) for information; the C.A.F. have an
    excellent network of huts ("refuges" and
    "chalets-refuges")
clock une horloge [or-lohj]
close¹: is it close? est-ce que c'est près d'ici?
    [esker say pray dee-see]
close² *(verb)* fermer [fair-may]
    closed fermé
    when do you close? quand est-ce que vous
    fermez?
cloth le tissu [tee-soo]
    (for wiping) un chiffon [shee-fon]
clothes les vêtements [vet-mon]
cloud un nuage [noo-ahj]

clutch l'embrayage [ōnbray-yahj]
  the clutch is slipping l'embrayage patine
  [. . . pah-teen]
coast la côte [koht]
  coast guard le garde-côte [gahrd-koht]
coat un manteau [mōn-toh]
  coatroom le vestiaire [vest-yair]
cockroach un cafard [kah-far]
coffee un café [kah-fay]
  black coffee café noir [. . . nwahr]
  coffee with hot milk café au lait [. . . oh lay]
» *TRAVEL TIP: if you want a small black coffee, ask
  for "un café petite tasse," for a large black
  coffee: "un café grande tasse;" "café au lait" is
  hot milk with hot black coffee; "café crème" is
  black coffee with a drop of milk or cream*
coin une pièce de monnaie [pee-yes der moh-nay]
  the coin is stuck la pièce est coincée
  [. . . kwān-say]
Coke *(drink)* un coca-cola
cold froid [frwah]
  I'm cold j'ai froid
  I've got a cold j'ai un rhume [jay ān room]
collapse: he's collapsed il s'est effondré
  [ayfōn-dray]
collar le col [kol]
» *TRAVEL TIP: continental sizes*

Continental	36	37	38	39	41	42	43
US	14	14½	15	15½ 16	16½ 17		

colleague un(une) collègue [koh-leg]
collect: I want to collect. . . je viens
  chercher. . . [. . . shair-shay]
  collect call une communication en PCV
  [kohmoo-nee-kahs-yōn ōn pay-say-vay]
collision une collision [kohleez-yōn]
color la couleur [koo-lerr]
  have you any other colors? est-ce que vous
  avez d'autres couleurs?
comb un peigne [pen]
come venir [ver-neer]

I come/we come from America je viens/nous venons d'Amérique [jer vee-yā̄n, noo ver-non . . .]

when is he coming? quand est-ce qu'il vient? [kōntesk-eel vee-yā̄n]

we came here yesterday nous sommes arrivés [noo somz ahree-vay] ici hier

come with me venez [ver-nay] avec moi

has he come back yet? est-ce qu'il est rentré?

come on! allons!

comfortable: it's not very comfortable ce n'est pas très confortable [. . . kōnfor-tahbl]

Common Market le Marché commun [marshay koh-mā̄n]

company une société [sohsyay-tay]

I like your company j'aime votre compagnie [jaym vohtr kōnpah-nee]

compartment *(train)* un compartiment [kōnpar-tee-mōn]

compass une boussole [boo-sohl]

compensation: I demand compensation je veux être dédommagé [. . . daydoh-mah-jay]

complain: I want to complain about . . . je désire réclamer au sujet de . . . [rayklah-may oh soo-jay der]

do you have a complaints book? est-ce que vous avez un registre [rer-jeestr] des réclamations?

complet no vacancies

completely complètement [kōnplet-mōn]

complicated compliqué [kōnplee-kay]

compliment: my compliments to the chef mes compliments [kōnplee-mōn] au chef

composter: prière de composter votre billet please punch your ticket here

compulsory: is it compulsory? est-ce que c'est obligatoire? [. . . ohblee-gah-twahr]

concern: I'm concerned about . . . je suis inquiet au sujet de . . . [jer swee ā̄nk-yay oh soo-jay der]

concert un concert
concierge caretaker
concussion une commotion cérébrale [kohmohs-yōn sayray-brahl]
condition: it's not in very good condition ce n'est pas en très bon état [ser nay pah ōn tray bohn ay-tah]
    what are your conditions? quelles sont vos conditions? [kel sōn voh kōn-dees-yōn]
condom le préservatif
confection ready-to-wear
conference une conférence [kōnfay-rōns]
confirm confirmer [kōnfeer-may]
congés vacation
congratulations félicitations [faylee-see-tahs-yōn]
conjunctivitis une conjonctivite [kōnjōnk-tee-veet]
connection *(train, etc.)* la correspondance [kohres-pōn-dōns]
connoisseur un connaisseur [kohnay-ser]
conscious conscient [kōns-yān]
consciousness: he's lost consciousness il a perdu connaissance [. . . kohnay-sāns]
consigne left luggage
constipation la constipation [kōnstee-pah-syōn]
consul le consul [kōn-sool]
consulate le consulat [kōnsoo-lah]
contact: how can I contact . . . ? comment est-ce que je peux contacter . . . ? [kohmōn esker jer per kōntak-tay]
    contact lenses les verrer [vair] de contact
contraceptive un contraceptif [kōntrah sep-teef]
convenient pratique [prah-teek]
cook cuire [kweer]
    it's not cooked ce n'est pas cuit [ser nay pah kwee]
    you are a good cook vous faites une excellente cuisine [voo fair oon exay-lōnt kwee-zeen]

are there any cooking facilities? est-ce qu'on peut y faire sa cuisine? [eskōn per ee fair ...]

cool frais (fraîche) [fray, fresh]

corkscrew le tire-bouchon [teerboo-shōn]

corn *(on foot)* un cor au pied [kohrohp-yay]

corner *(bend)* un virage [vee-rahj]

can we have a corner table? est-ce qu'on peut avoir une table d'angle? [eskōn per ah-vwahr oon tahbl dōngl]

cornflakes des cornflakes

correct correct

cosmetics des produits de beauté [prohdwee der boh-tay]

cost: what does it cost? combien ça coûte [kōnb-yān sah koot]

cot un lit d'enfant [lee dōn-fōn]

cotton du coton [koh-tōn]

cough la toux [too]

cough drops des bonbons [bōnbōn] pour la toux

cough mixture un sirop [see-roh] pour la toux

could: could you please ...? est-ce que vous pouvez ...? [esker voo poo-vay]

could I have ...? est-ce que je peux avoir ...? [esker jer per ah-vwahr]

we couldn't ... nous n'avons pas pu ... [noo nah-vōn pah poo]

country un pays [payee]

in the country à la campagne [ah lah kōn-pan]

couple: a couple of ... quelques ... [kelk]

courier l'accompagnateur [ahkōn-pahn-yah-terr]

course: first course l'entrée [ōn-tray]

main course le plat principal [plah prānsee-pal]

meat course le plat de viande [... vee-yōnd]

of course naturellement [nahtoo-rel-mōn]

court: I'll take you to court je vais vous poursuivre en justice [... poorsweevr-ōn-joos-tees]

cousin: my cousin mon cousin [koo-zān]

cover *(verb)* couvrir [koo-vreer]
  keep him well covered couvrez-le bien
  cover charge le couvert [koo-vair]
cow une vache [vash]
crab un crabe [krahb]
craft shop une boutique d'artisanat
  [. . . artee-zah-nah]
crash: there's been a crash il y a eu une
  collision [eelyah oo oon kohleez-yōn]
  crash helmet un casque [kahsk]
crazy: you're crazy vous êtes fou (folle)
cream de la crème [kraym]
credit card une carte de crédit [. . . kray-dee]
crêperie pancake shop
crib une crèche [kraysh]
cross *(noun)* une croix [krwah]
  (verb) traverser [trahvair-say]
crossroads un carrefour [kar-foor]
crowded: it's crowded il y a beaucoup de
  monde [eelyah bohkoo-der-mōnd]
cruise une croisière [krwahz-yair]
crutch une béquille [bay-kee]
cry: don't cry ne pleurez pas [pler-ray . . .]
cufflink un bouton de manchette [boo-tōn der
  mōn-shet]
cup une tasse [tahs]
  a cup of coffee/tea un café/thé [kah-fay, tay]
cupboard une armoire [arm-wahr]
curry un plat au curry [plah oh ker-ree]
curtains les rideaux [ree-doh]
cushion un coussin [koo-sān]
Customs la douane [dwahn]
cut couper [koo-pay]
  I've cut myself je me suis coupé [jer mer swee
  koo-pay]
cycle: can we cycle there? est-ce qu'on peut y
  aller à bicyclette? [eskōn per ee ah-lay ah
  beesee-klet]
cyclist un cycliste [see-kleest]
cylinder un cylindre [see-lāndr]

cylinder head gasket un joint de culasse [jwan der koo-lass]

damage: I'll pay for the damage je rembourserai les dégâts [jer ronboor-ser-ray lay day-gah]

it's damaged c'est abîmé [. . . ahbee-may]

damp humide [oo-mid]

dames ladies' toilets

dance: is there a dance? est-ce qu'il y a une soirée dansante? [eskeelyah oon swah-ray don-sont]

would you like to dance? voulez-vous danser? [voolay-voo don-say]

dangerous dangereux [donj-rer]

dark *(color)* foncé [fon-say]

dark blue bleu foncé [bler . . .]

when does it get dark? quand est-ce que la nuit tombe? [kontesker lah nwee-tonb]

darling: my darling *(to man)* mon chéri [mon shar-ree]

(to lady) ma chérie [mah . . .]

dashboard le tableau de bord [tahbloh der bor]

date *(fruit)* une datte [dat]

(time) la date [dat]

what's the date today? quelle est la date d'aujourd'hui? [kel ay lah dat dohjoor-dwee]

can we make a date? est-ce que nous pouvons fixer un rendez-vous? [esker noo poovon feexay an ronday-voo]

it's the 1st of February c'est le premier février [prerm-yay . . .]

on the 2nd of February le deux février *(NB: except for the 1st of the month, use "deux", "trois", etc. and not "deuxième", etc.)*

in 1983 en dix-neuf cent quatre-vingt trois [deez-ner-son kah-trer-van trwah]

daughter: my daughter ma fille [fee]

day un jour [joor]

by day de jour

the day after le lendemain [londer-man]

the day before la veille [vay]

dead mort [mor]

deaf sourd [soor]

deal un marché [mahr-shay]

   it's a deal! d'accord! [dah-kor]

   will you deal with it? est-ce que vous pouvez vous en charger? [esker voo poovay voo zōn shar-jay]

dealer: the Ford dealer le concessionnaire Ford [kōnsess-yoh-nair . . .]

dear cher [shair]; *see* **letter**

December: in December en décembre [day-sōnbr]

deck le pont [pōn]

   deckchair une chaise longue [shayz lōng]

declare: I have nothing to declare je n'ai rien à déclarer [jer nay ree-yān nah dayklah-ray]

deep: is it deep? est-ce que c'est profond? [esker say proh-fōn]

defect: there's a defect c'est défectueux [dayfek-too-er]

défense d'entrer no entry

delay un retard [rer-tahr]

   the flight was delayed le vol a eu du retard [ler vol ah oo doo . . .]

deliberately exprès [ex-pray]

delicate délicat [daylee-kah]

delicatessen une épicerie fine [ay-pees-ree-feen]

delicious délicieux [daylees-yer]

   that was a delicious meal ce repas était délicieux [ser rerpah aytay daylees-yer]

deliver livrer [lee-vray]

delivery *(of goods)* la livraison [leevray-zōn]

   (of mail) la distribution [deestree-boos-yōn]

deluxe de luxe [der-looks]

democratic démocratique [daymoh-krah-teek]

demonstration une démonstration [. . . -trahs-yōn]

   (political, etc.) une manifestation [. . . -tahs-yōn]

dent une bosse [boss]

....

you've dented my car vous avez endommagé
ma carosserie [. . . ōndoh-mah-jay . . .]
dentist un dentiste [dōn-teest]
YOU MAY HEAR…
ouvrez! *open wide,* rincez! *you can rinse now*
dentures un dentier [dōnt-yay]
deny: I deny it ce n'est pas vrai [ser nay pah
vray]
deodorant un déodorant [day-oh-doh-rōn]
dépannage towing service
departure le départ [day-par]
departure gate la salle d'embarquement
[sahl dōnbar-ker-mōn]
depend: it depends (on) ça dépend
[day-pōn] (de)
deposit *(down payment)* un acompte [ah-kōnt]
(security) une caution [kohs-yōn]
(on bottle, etc.) la consigne [kōn-seen]
do I have to pay a deposit? est-ce qu'il faut
verser un acompte? [eskeel foh vair-say ān
ah-kōnt]
depressed déprimé [daypree-may]
depth la profondeur [prohfōn-derr]
desperate: I'm desperate for a drink je meurs
de soif [jer merr der swahf]
dessert un dessert [day-sair]
» *TRAVEL TIP: always served after cheese*
destination la destination [destee-nahs-yōn]
detergent un détergent [daytair-jōn]
detour un détour [day-toor]
devalued dévalué [dayvah-loo-ay]
develop: could you develop these? est-ce que
vous pouvez me développer [dayv-loh-pay] ces
films?
diabetic diabétique [dee-yah-bay-teek]
dial le cadran [kah-drōn]
dialing code l'indicatif [āndee-kah-teef]
dial tone la tonalité [tohnah-lee-tay]
diamond un diamant [dee-yah-mōn]
diapers les couches [koosh]

disposable diapers des couches à jeter [... ah jer-tay]

diaper liners les protège-couches [proh-tayj-koosh]

diarrhea: have you got something for diarrhea? est-ce que vous avez quelque chose pour la diarrhée? [... kel-ker shohz poor lah dee-yah-ray]

diary un agenda [ahjon-dah]

dictionary un dictionnaire [deeks-yoh-nair]

didn't see **not**

die mourir [moo-reer]

he's dying il est mourant [moo-ron]

diesel *(fuel)* du gas-oil [gahz-wahl]

diet un régime [ray-jeem]

I'm on a diet je suis au régime [jer swee...]

different différent [deefay-ron]

can I have a different room? est-ce que je peux avoir une autre chambre? [esker jer per ah-vwahr oon ohtr shonbr]

difficult difficile [deefee-seel]

digestion la digestion [deejest-yon]

dinghy *(rubber)* un canot pneumatique [kah-noh pnermah-teek]

(sailing) un dériveur [dayree-verr]

dining car la voiture-restaurant [vwah-toor...]

dining room la salle à manger [sahlah-mon-jay]

dinner le dîner [dee-nay]

dinner jacket un smoking

direct: does it go direct? est-ce que c'est direct? [... dee-rekt]

directory *(telephone)* l'annuaire [ah-nwair] du téléphone

dirty sale [sahl]

disabled handicapé [ondee-kah-pay]

disappear disparaître [deespah-raitr]

disappointing décevant [days-von]

disco une discothèque [-tek]

discount un rabais [rah-bay]

disgusting dégoûtant [daygoo-ton]

dish un plat [plah]

....

dishwashing liquid du détergent pour la vaisselle [daytair-jon poor lah vay-sel]
dishonest malhonnête [mahloh-net]
disinfectant un désinfectant [dayzan-fek-ton]
distance la distance [dees-tons]
  in the distance au loin [lwan]
distilled water de l'eau distillée [oh deestee-lay]
distress signal un signal de détresse [seen-yal der day-tres]
distributor *(on car)* le delco [del-koh]
district le quartier [kart-yay]
disturb déranger [day-ron-jay]
  the noise is disturbing us le bruit [brwee] nous dérange
diving board le plongeoir [plon-jwahr]
divorced: I'm divorced je suis divorcé [jer swee deevohr-say]
do faire [fair]
  how do you do? comment allez-vous? [koh-mont ah-lay voo]
  can I do this? est-ce que je peux faire ça? [esker jer per fair sah]
  what are you doing tonight? qu'est-ce que vous faites ce soir? [kesker voo fayt ser swahr]
  how do you do it? comment est-ce que vous faites? [koh-mont esker voo fayt]
  what did you do? qu'est-ce que vous avez fait? [kesker vooz ah-vay fay]
  will you do it for me? est-ce que vous pouvez le faire pour moi?
  I've never done it before je n'ai jamais fait ça [. . . jah-may fay sah]
  I was doing 60 kph je roulais à soixante [jer roo-lay ah swah-sont]
doctor un docteur [dok-terr]
  I need a doctor j'ai besoin d'un docteur [jay ber-zwan]
  YOU MAY HEAR...
  est-ce que vous avez déjà eu ça? *have you had this before?*

où est-ce que ça vous fait mal? *where does it hurt?*

est-ce que vous prenez des médicaments? *are you taking any drugs?*

prenez-en deux, trois fois par jour/aux heures des repas *take two, three times a day/at meal times*

document un document [dohkoo-mōn]

dog un chien [shee-yān]

don't *see* **not**

    don't! non! [nōn]

door la porte [pohrt]

dosage la dose [dohz]

douane Customs

double double [doobl]

    double room une chambre pour deux [shōnbr poor der]

    double whiskey un double whisky

douche shower

Dover Douvres [doovr]

down en bas [ōn-bah]

    downstairs au rez-de-chaussée [rayd-shoh-say]

    get down! descendez! [day-sōn-day]

drain *(in street)* un égout [ay-goo]

    (in bathroom) le tuyau d'ecoulement [twee-yoh daykool-mōn]

dress une robe [rohb]

    I'm not dressed je ne suis pas habillé [. . . pahz-ahbee-yay]

» *TRAVEL TIP: sizes*

US	8	10	12	14	16	18	20
France	36	38	40	42	44	46	48

dressing *(on wound)* un pansement [pōns-mōn]

    (in salad, etc.) l'assaisonnement [ahsay-zon-mōn]

drink *(verb)* boire [bwahr]

    something to drink quelque chose à boire

    would you like a drink? désirez-vous [dayzee-ray voo] boire quelque chose?

    I don't drink je ne bois pas d'alcool [jer ner bwah pah dal-kol]

I had too much to drink last night j'ai trop bu hier soir [jay troh boo . . .]

is the water drinkable? est-ce que l'eau est potable? [esker loh ay poh-tahbl]

drive conduire [kon-dweer]

I've been driving all day j'ai roulé [roo-lay] toute la journée

I was driving c'est moi qui conduisais [kondwee-zay]

driver le conducteur [kondook-terr]

(taxi) le chauffeur [shoh-ferr]

driving license le permis [pair-mee] de conduire

» *TRAVEL TIP: driving in France pay attention to "priorité": as a rule cars coming from the right have right of way unless you are in "passage protégé", when you have the right of way; always have your license ready*

droguerie drugstore

drown: he's drowning il se noie [eel ser nwah]

drug un médicament [maydee-kah-mon]

(narcotic, etc.) la drogue [drog]

he is taking drugs il prend [pron] des médicaments

drugstore une pharmacie [farmah-see]

» *TRAVEL TIP: often with green cross sign; most will make up a prescription; address of pharmacists on all-night or Sunday duty (pharmacie de garde) in local paper or on door of every "pharmacie"*

drunk ivre [eevr]

dry *(adjective)* sec (sèche) [sek, sesh]

(verb) sécher [say-shay]

dry-clean nettoyer à sec [naytwah-yay ah sek]

dry cleaner une teinturerie [tantoor-ree]

due: when is the bus due? quand est-ce que le bus doit arriver? [kont esker ler boos dwaht ahree-vay]

during pendant [pon-don]

dust la poussière [poos-yair]

duty-free hors taxe [ohr-tax]

duty-free shop une boutique hors taxe

dynamo la dynamo [deenah-moh]
each chaque [shahk]
  can we have one each? est-ce que nous
  pouvons en avoir un chacun? [. . . oñ
  nah-vwahr uñ shah-kuñ]
  how much are they each? combien est-ce
  qu'ils sont la piéce? [koñb-yuñ eskeel soñ lah
  pee-yes]
ear l'oreille [oh-ray]
  I have an earache j'ai des douleurs [doo-lerr]
  à l'oreille
early tôt [toh]
  we want to leave a day earlier nous voulons
  partir un jour plus tôt [noo voo-loñ pahr-teer
  uñ joor ploo toh]
earring une boucle d'oreille [bookl doh-ray]
east l'est [est]
easy facile [fah-seel]
Easter Pâques [pahk]
  at Easter à Pâques
  Easter Monday le lundi [luñ-dee] de Pâques
eat manger [moñ-jay]
  something to eat quelque chose [kel-ker
  shohz] à manger
eau potable *drinking water*
egg un oeuf [erf]
eggplant une aubergine [ohbair-jeen]
Eire la République d'Irlande [. . . eer-loñd]
either: either this one or that one ou celui-ci
  ou celui-là [oo serlwee-see oo serlwee-lah]
  I don't like either aucun des deux ne me
  plait [oh-kuñ day der . . .]
  either would do ou l'un ou l'autre fera
  l'affaire [oo luñ oo lohtr . . .]
elastic élastique [aylass-teek]
elbow le coude [kood]
electric électrique [aylek-treek]
  electric blanket une couverture chauffante
  [koovair-toor shoh-foñt]
  electric heater un radiateur électrique
  [rahd-yah-ter aylek-trik]

electrical outlet une prise de courant [preez der koo-rōn]

electricity l'électricité [aylek-tree-see-tay]

» *TRAVEL TIP: 220v the rule but 110v also in use: do check; 2-pin plugs widely used, also 3-pin plug; get an adaptor before you go, or buy a "prise électrique" in a local supermarket*

électro-ménager electrical appliances

elegant élégant [aylay-gōn]

elevator l'ascenseur
   the elevator isn't working l'ascenseur ne marche pas [lahsōn-serr ner marsh pah]

else: something else quelque chose d'autre [kelker-shoz dohtr]
   somebody else quelqu'un d'autre [kelkān dohtr]
   somewhere else ailleurs [ah-yerr]
   who/what else? qui/quoi d'autre? [kee, kwah dohtr]
   or else . . . sinon . . . [see-nōn]

embarrassed gêné [jay-nay]

embarrassing embarrassant [ōnbah-rah-sōn]

embassy l'ambassade [ōnbah-sad]

emergency une urgence [oor-jōns]
   help me please aidez-moi s'il vous plaît [ayday-mwah see voo play]

» *TRAVEL TIP: emergency numbers on all telephone dials; "pompiers" fire brigade; "Police Secours" police*

empty vide [veed]

enclose: I enclose with my letter . . . je joins à ma lettre . . . [jer jwān ah ma laitr]

end la fin [fān]
   when does it end? quand est-ce que ça finit? [kōn tesker sah fee-nee]

enfants children

engaged *(to be married)* fiancé [fee-ōn-say]

engine le moteur [moh-terr]
   engine trouble des ennuis mécaniques [ōn-nwee maykah-neek]

England l'Angleterre [ōngler-tair]

English anglais [oⁿ-glay]

enjoy: I enjoyed it very much j'ai beaucoup aimé [jay boh-koo ay-may]
I enjoyed the meal j'ai très bien mangé [jay trayb-yaⁿ moⁿ-jay]

enlargement *(photo)* un agrandissement [ahgroⁿ-dees-moⁿ]

enormous énorme [ay-norm]

enough assez [ah-say]
that's not big enough ce n'est pas assez grand
I don't have enough money je n'ai pas assez d'argent
thank you, that's enough merci, ça suffit [soo-fee]

entertainment *(shows, etc.)* les attractions [ahtraks-yoⁿ]

entrance l'entrée [oⁿ-tray]

entry l'entrée [oⁿ-tray]
entry permit un laisser-passer [laysay-pah-say]

envelope une enveloppe [oⁿv-lop]

equipment *(sports, etc.)* le matériel [mahtayr-yel]

error une erreur [ay-rer]

escalator un escalier roulant [eskahl-yay roor-loⁿ]

especially spécialement [spays-yahl-moⁿ]

essential essentiel [aysoⁿs-yel]

Europe l'Europe [er-rop]
European européen [er-roh-pay-aⁿ]

evacuate évacuer [ayvah-kooay]

even même [maim]

evening le soir [swahr]
in the evening le soir
evening dress la robe de soirée [rob der swah-ray]

ever: have you ever been to ...? est-ce que vous êtes déjà allé à ...? [esker voo zait day-jah ahlay ah]

every chaque [shahk]

every day chaque jour [shahk joor]
everyone chacun [shah-kūn], tous *(plural)* [toos]
everything tout [too]
everywhere partout [pahr-too]
evidence: to give evidence témoigner [taymwahn-yay]
exact exact [ayg-zakt]
example un exemple [ayg-zōnpl]
  for example par exemple
excellent excellent [ayksay-lōn]
except: except me à part moi [ah-par . . .]
excess *(insurance)* la franchise [frōn-sheez]
  excess baggage un excédent de bagages [ayksay-dōn der bah-gahj]
exchange *(money)* le change [shōnj]
  exchange rate le taux de change [toh der shōnj]
excursion une excusion [exkoors-yōn]
excuse me pardon Monsieur *(or Madame, Mademoiselle)* [pahr-dōn mers-yer, mah-dam, mahder-mwah-zel]
exhaust *(car)* le tuyau d'échappement [twee-oh dayshap-mōn]
exhausted épuisé [aypwee-zay]
exhibition une exposition [expoh-zees-yōn]
exhibitor un exposant [expoh-zōn]
exit la sortie [sohr-tee]
expect: she's expecting elle attend un bébé [el ah-tōn ān bay-bay]
  I'm expected je suis attendu [jer swee ahtōn-doo]
expenses les dépenses [day-pōns]
  it's on an expense account ça va sur la note de frais [sah vah soor lah not der fray]
expensive cher [shair]
expert un spécialiste [spays-yah-leest]
explain expliquer [explee-kay]
export exporter [expohr-tay]
exposure: 24 exposure film un film de vingt-quatre poses [. . . pohz]

express: I'd like to send it express j'aimerais
l'envoyer par exprès [jaym-ray lōnvwah-yay
pahr ex-pres]

extra: is it extra? est-ce que c'est en
supplément? [esker say ōn sooplay-mōn]
  an extra blanket une couverture de plus [oon
koovair-toor der ploos]

eye l'oeil [er-ee]
  the eyes les yeux [yer]
  eye drops une lotion [lohs-yōn] pour les yeux
  eyeshadow le fard à paupières [fahr ah
pohp-yair]
  eyewitness un témoin oculaire [tay-mwān
ohkoo-lair]

fabric un tissu [tee-soo]

face le visage [vee-zahj]

factory une fabrique [fah-brik]

Fahrenheit *see* **centigrade**

faint: she's fainted elle s'est évanouie [el sayt
ayvah-nwee]

fair une foire [fwahr]
  that's not fair ce n'est pas juste [ser nay pah
joost]

faithfully *see* **letter**

fake faux (fausse) [foh, fohs]

fall tomber [tōn-bay]
  he's fallen il est tombé

false faux (fausse) [foh, fohs]
  false teeth un dentier [dōnt-yay]

family la famille [fah-mee]
  do you have any family? est-ce que vous
avez des enfants? [esker voo zay-vay day
zōnfōn]

fan *(in car, room, etc.)* le ventilateur [vōntee-
lah-terr]
  (supporter) un supporter [soopohr-tair]
  fan belt la courroie de ventilateur
[koo-rwah . . .]

far loin [lwān]
  is it far? est-ce que c'est loin? [esker say
lwān]

how far is it? c'est à quelle distance d'ici? [say ah kel dees-tōns dee-see]

fare *(travel)* le prix du billet [pree doo bee-yay]

half fare le demi-tarif [der-mee tah-reef]

full fare le plein tarif [plān ...]

farm une ferme [fairm]

farther plus loin [ploo lwān]

fashion la mode [mod]

fashion shop une boutique de mode

fast *(adjective)* rapide [rah-peed]

don't speak so fast ne parlez pas si vite [ner pahr-lay pah see veet]

fat gros [groh]

(on meat) du gras [grah]

father: my father mon père [pair]

fathom une brasse *(1.83 m)*

faucet le robinet [rohbee-nay]

fault un défaut [day-foh]

it's not my fault ce n'est pas de ma faute [ser nay pahd mah foht]

favorite préferé [prayfay-ray]

February: in February en février [fayvree-ay]

fed up: I'm fed up j'en ai assez [jōn nay ah-say]

fee: what's the fee? combien ça coûte? [kōnb-yān sah koot]

feel: I feel cold/hot j'ai froid/chaud [jay frwah, shoh]

I don't feel well je ne me sens pas bien [jern mer sōn pah bee-yān]

I feel ill je me sens mal [jerm sōn mal]

I feel sick j'ai mal au coeur [jay mal oh kerr]

I feel like *(I want)* j'ai envie de [jay ōn-vee der]

felt-tip pen un stylo-feutre [steeloh-fertr]

femmes women

fermé closed

ferry le ferry-boat [fairee-boht]

festival un festival [festee-val]

fever la fièvre [fee-yaivr]

I am feverish j'ai de la fièvre [jay ...]

he's got a fever il a de la température

few: few people peu de gens [per der jōn]
    a few days quelques jours [kel-ker joor]
    only a few seulement quelques uns [serl-mōn kelker-zān]
fiancé: my fiancé mon fiancé [fee-yōn-say]
    my fiancée ma fiancée
field un champ [shōn]
fig une figue [fig]
fight: there's been a fight il y a eu une bagarre [eelyahoo oon bah-gahr]
figure *(digit)* un chiffre [sheefr]
    I'm watching my figure je surveille ma ligne [jer soor-vay mah leen]
fill remplir [rōn-pleer]
    fill her up faites le plein [fait ler plān]
    do I have to fill in a form? est-ce que je dois remplir un formulaire? [esker jer dwah rōn-pleerr ān fohrmoo-lair]
fillet un filet [fee-lay]
filling *(in tooth)* un plombage [plōn-bahj]
film un film
    I would like a 35 mm film j'aimerais un film 24 × 36 [jaym-ray ān film vānt-kat trōnt-sees]
    a color/b & w film un film couleur/noir et blanc [. . . koo-lerr, nwahr ay blōn]
    a 20 exposure film un film de vingt poses [. . . der vān pohz]
filter un filtre [feeltr]
find trouver [troo-vay]
    if you find it si vous le (la) trouvez [see voo ler troo-vay]
    I've found a . . . j'ai trouvé un . . . [jay . . .]
fine: the weather is fine il fait beau temps [eel fay boh tōn]
    a 50 francs fine une amende de cinquante francs [oon ah-mōnd der . . .]
    OK, that's fine d'accord, ça va bien [dah-kor sah vah bee-yān]
finger le doigt [dwah]
    fingernail un ogle [ōngl]
finish finir [fee-neer]

....

I haven't finished je n'ai pas fini [jer nay pah
fee-nee]
fire un feu [fer]
(blaze: house on fire, etc.) un incendie
[ānsōn-dee]
fire! au feu! [oh fer]
can we light a fire here? est-ce qu'on peut
faire du feu ici? [eskōn per fair doo fer ee-see]
call the fire department appelez les
pompiers [ap-lay lay pōnp-yay]
» TRAVEL TIP: *the fire department number
"pompiers" is on all telephone dials*
fire extinguisher un extincteur [ex-tānk-terr]
fireworks un feu d'artifice [fer dahrtee-fees]
firm une entreprise [ōntrer-preez]
first premier [prerm-yay]
I was first j'étais le premier
first aid les premiers secours [. . . ser-koor]
first aid kit une trousse [troos] de premiers
secours
first name le prénom [pray-nōn]
fish du poisson [pwah-sōn]
fish market une poissonnerie [pwahson-ree]
fishing le pêche [paish]
fishing rod une canne [kan] à pêche
» TRAVEL TIP: *if you want to go fishing you will
need a special permit, "le permis de pêche";
inquire at the "syndicat d'initiative"*
fit *(healthy)* en bonne condition physique [ōn
bonn kōndees-yōn fee-zeek]
it doesn't fit me ça ne me va pas [sann mer
vah pah]
fix: can you fix it? *(repair)* est-ce que vous
pouvez le réparer? [esker voo poo-vay ler
raypah-ray]
(arrange) est-ce que vous pouvez arranger ça?
[. . . ahrōnjay sah]
flag un drapeau [drah-poh]
flannel un gant de toilette [gōn der twah-let]
flash *(photo)* un flash
flashcube une ampoule de flash [ōn-pool . . .]

flat plat [plah]

   I've got a flat *(tire)* j'ai un pneu à plat [jay
a̅n̅ pner . . .]

   can you repair a flat? est-ce que vous pouvez
réparer une crevaison? [esker voo poovay
raypah-ray oon krervay-zo̅n̅]

flavor la saveur [sah-verr]

fleas des puces [poos]

flies *(on trousers)* la braguette [brah-get]

flight un vol

flippers des palmes [pahlm]

float flotter

floor: on which floor? à quel étage? [ah kel
ay-tahj]

   the ground floor le rez-de-chaussée
[rayd-shoh-say]

   the top floor le dernier étage [dairn-yay . . .]

   on the floor par terre [par tair]

» *TRAVEL TIP: Europeans call the second floor the
first floor, the third floor the second floor, etc.*

flowers des fleurs [flerr]

   bunch of flowers un bouquet [boo-kay]

flu la grippe [grip]

fly *(insect)* la mouche [moosh]

   we flew here nous sommes venus en avion
[noo som ver-noo o̅n̅n̅ ahv-yo̅n̅]

foggy: it's foggy il y a du brouillard [eelyah doo
broo-yahr]

fold plier [plee-yay]

follow suivre [sweevr]

food la nourriture [nooree-toor]

   food store un magasin d'alimentation
[mahgah za̅n̅ dahleemo̅n̅-tahs-yo̅n̅]

   food poisoning une intoxication alimentaire
[a̅n̅tohksee-kahs-yo̅n̅ ahlee-o̅n̅-tair]

foot le pied [pee-yay]

» *TRAVEL TIP: 1 foot = 30.1 cm = 0.3 m*

for pour

   we've been here for a week nous sommes ici
depuis une semaine [noo som zee-see
der-pwee . . .]

forbidden interdit [ān̄tair-dee]
foreign étranger [aytrōn̄-jay]
   foreigner un étranger
forest une forêt [foh-ray]
forget oublier [ooblee-yay]
   I've forgotten... j'ai oublié... [jay...]
   don't forget n'oubliez pas [nooblee-yay pah]
fork une fourchette [foor-shet]
form un formulaire [fohrmoo-lair]
formal officiel [ohfees-yel]
fortnight: for a fortnight pour deux semaines
   [... der ser-mayn]
fortunate: we were fortunate nous avons eu de
   la chance [noo zah-vōn̄ oo der lah shōn̄s]
   fortunately heureusement [er-rerz-mōn̄]
forward en avant [ōn̄ nah-vōn̄]
   could you forward my mail? est-ce que vous
   pouvez faire suivre mon courrier? [... fair
   sweevr mōn̄ koor-yay]
   here is a forwarding address voici l'adresse
   où envoyer le courrier [lah-dress oo
   ōn̄vwah-yay...]
foundation *(makeup)* un fond de teint [fōn̄ der
   tān̄]
fountain une fontaine [fōn̄-tain]
fracture une fracture [frak-toor]
fragile fragile [frah-jeel]
franc un franc [frōn̄]
   Swiss francs des francs suisses [... sweess]
   Belgian francs des francs belges [... belj]
France la France [frōn̄s]
free libre [leebr]
freeway l'autoroute [ohtoh-root]
freezer un congélateur [kōn̄jay-lah-terr]
French français [frōn̄say]
   Frenchman un Français
   Frenchwoman une Française [frōn̄-sayz]
   I don't speak French je ne parle pas français
   [jer ner pahrl pah frōn̄-say]
   french fries des frites [freet]
fresh frais (fraîche) [fray, fraish]

**freshen up: I'd like to go and freshen
up** j'aimerais faire un peu de toilette [jaym-
ray fair a̅n̅ per der twah-let]
Friday vendredi [vo̅n̅drer-dee]
fried frit [free]
   fried egg un oeuf sur le plat [a̅n̅ nerf soor ler
   plah]
   nothing fried pas de fritures [pah der
   free-toor]
friend un ami [ah-mee]
friendly sympathique [sa̅n̅pah-teek]
from de [der]
   where is it from? d'où est-ce que ça vient?
   [doo esker sah vee-ya̅n̅]
front: in front (of) devant [der-vo̅n̅]
frost le gel [jel]
   frostbite des gelures [jer-loor]
frozen gelé [jer-lay]
   frozen food des aliments surgelés [ahlee-mo̅n̅
   soorjer-lay]
fruit des fruits [frwee]
   fruit juice un jus de fruits [joo der frwee]
   fruit salad une macédoine de fruits
   [mahsay-dwahn]
fry frire [freer]
   frying pan une poêle [pwahl]
full plein [pla̅n̅]
fumeurs: non-fumeurs no smoking
fun: it's fun c'est amusant [sayt ahmoo-zo̅n̅]
   we had fun nous nous sommes bien amusés
   [noo noo som bee-ya̅n̅ ahmoo-zay]
funny drôle [drohl]
furniture les meubles [merbl]
further plus loin [ploo lwa̅n̅]
fuse un fusible [foo-zeebl]
fuss: I don't want any fuss je ne veux pas
   d'histoires [jer ner ver pah dees-twahr]
future: in the future à l'avenir [ah lahv-neer]
gale une tempête [to̅n̅-pet]
gallon un gallon [gah-lon]
» *TRAVEL TIP: 1 gallon = 4.55 liters*

gallstone un calcul biliaire [kal-kool beel-yair]
galoshes des bottes de caoutchouc [bot der kahoo-tshoo]
gambling: I like gambling j'aime le jeu [jaym ler jer]
game un jeu [jer]
garage un garage [gah-rahj]
» *TRAVEL TIP: ask for "un devis" (estimate), "une facture détaillée" (itemized bill), "la durée des réparations" (estimated time for repairs); avoid highway garages whenever possible*
garden un jardin [jahr-dān]
garlic l'ail [as "eye"]
gas le gaz [gahz]
  gas cylinder une bouteille de gaz [boo-tay ...]
gasoline de l'essence [ay-sōns]
  gas station une station-service [stahs-yon-sair-vees]
  gas gauge la jauge [johj] à essence
  gas can le jerrycan d'essence
  gas tank le réservoir
  YOU MAY SEE OR HEAR...
  super [soo-par] *super*
  ordinaire [ohrdee-nair] *regular*
  normale [nor-mahl] *regular*
  give me 50F worth of super donnez-moi pour cinquante francs de super [doh-nay-mwah poor sān-kōnt frōn der soo-pair]
» *TRAVEL TIP: the pump attendant will expect a tip if he gives your windshield a wipe; routine checks such as "les niveaux" (oil and battery level) can be costly*
gasket un joint [jwān]
gauge une jauge [johj]
gear *(in car)* la vitesse [vee-tess]
  (equipment) le matériel [mahtayr-yel]
  in 1st gear en première vitesse [prerm-yair ...]
  gearbox trouble des ennuis avec la boîte de vitesses [dayz-ōn-nwee ah-vek lah bwaht der vee-tess]

gear shift le levier de vitesses [lerv-yay]
I can't get it into gear je n'arrive pas à
mettre la vitesse [jer nah-reev pah ah
maitr . . .]
gentleman: the gentleman here told me ... ce
monsieur m'a dit ... [ser mers-yer mah dee]
genuine véritable [vayree-tahbl]
German allemand [al-mōn]
Germany l'Allemagne [al-mann]
gesture un geste [jest]
» TRAVEL TIP: *the French use their hands more
than Americans do when they speak; be
prepared to shake hands as often as required*
get: will you get me a ...? est-ce que vous
pouvez me chercher un ... [esker voo poovay
mer shair-shay]
will you come and get me? est-ce que vous
pouvez venir me chercher? [esker voo poovay
ver-neer mer shair-shay]
could you go and get ...? est-ce que vous
pouvez aller chercher ...?
how do I get to ...? comment est-ce qu'on
peut aller à ...? [koh mōn eskōn per ah-lay ah]
we got here last night nous sommes arrivés
hier soir [noo somz ahreevay ...]
when can I get it back? quand est-ce que je
peux le ravoir? [kōntesker jer per ler
rah-vwahr]
when do we get back? quand est-ce que nous
rentrons? [... rōn-trōn]
get down descendre [day-sōndr]
when do I get off? où est-ce que je dois
descendre? [wesker jer dwah day-sōndr]
I can't get in je ne peux pas entrer [jern per
pah ōn-tray]
get out sortir [sohr-teer]
I get up at 7 je me lève à sept heures [jer mer
laiv ...]
gin du gin [djeen]
gin and tonic un gin and tonic
girl une fille [fee]

my girlfriend mon amie [ah-mee]
NB *"fille" also means "daughter"; "jeune fille"*
[jern . . .] *is used for unmarried girl*
gîtes ruraux *housekeeping accommodation*
gîtes d'étape *dormitory accommodation (for hikers, etc.)*
give donner [doh-nay]
  will you give me . . . ? est-ce que vous pouvez me donner . . . ? [esker voo poovay mer doh-nay]
  can you give me back . . . ? est-ce que vous pouvez me rendre . . . ? [. . . mer rōndr]
glad: I'm glad (to . . .) je suis content (de . . .) [jer swee kōn-tōn . . .]
glass un verre [vair]
  glass of water/of wine un verre d'eau/de vin [vairdoh, vairder-vān]
glasses *(eye)* des lunettes [loo-net]
  my glasses mes lunettes [loo-net]
gloves des gants [gōn]
glue de la colle [kol]
go aller [ah-lay]
  he's/they are going there on Sunday il y va/ils y vont dimanche [eel ee vah, eel zee vōn]
  where are you going? où allez-vouz? [oo ah-lay voo]
  I'm/we are going there tomorrow j'y vais/nous y allons demain [jee vay, noo zee ah-lōn . . .]
  he's gone il est parti [eelay pahr-tee]
  we went to Italy last year nous sommes allés en Italie l'année dernière [noo somz ah-lay . . .]
  when does the bus go? quand est-ce que le bus part? [kōnt esker ler boos pahr]
  go down descendre [day-sōndr]
  go in entrer [ōn-tray]
  go on continuer [kōntee-nway]
  go out sortir [sorh-teer]
  go up monter [mōn-tay]
goal un but [boot]

goat une chèvre [shaivr]
  goat cheese du fromage de chèvre
  [froh-mahj...]
God Dieu [dee-yer]
goggles des lunettes protectrices [loo-net
  prohtek-trees]
gold: a gold chain une chaînette en or
  [shay-net ōnn ohr]
  YOU MAY HEAR...
  c'est plaqué- or *it's gold plated*
golf le golf [gohlf]
  golf course un terrain [tay-rān] de golf
good bon [bōn]
  good! très bien! [tray-bee-yān]
  be good! soyez sage! [sway-yay sahj]
  good luck! bonne chance! [bonn shōns]
  good morning, good afternoon bonjour
  (Monsieur *or* Madame *or* Mademoiselle)
  [bōn-joor mers-yer, mah-dam, mad-mwah-zel]
  good evening bonsoir (Monsieur *or* Madame
  or Mademoiselle) [bōn-swahr...]
  good night bonne nuit! [bonn nwee]
  Good Friday le Vendredi saint [vōndrer-dee
  sān]
good-bye au revoir! [oh rer-vwahr]
gooseberries des groseilles à maquereau
  [groh-zay ah mak-roh]
gram un gramme [gram]
  » *TRAVEL TIP: 100 grams = 3½ oz*
grand grand [grōn]
  my grandfather mon grand-père [grōn-pair]
  my grandmother ma grand-mère [grōn-mair]
  my grandchildren mes petits-enfants
  my grandson mon petit-fils [pertee-fees]
  my granddaughter ma petite-fille
  [perteet-fee]
grape un raisin [ray-zān]
  grapes du raisin
grapefruit un pamplemousse [pōnpler-moos]
  grapefruit juice un jus [joo] de pamplemousse
grass l'herbe [airb]

grateful: I'm very grateful to you je vous suis très reconnaissant [jer voo swee tray rerkoh-nay-son]

gratuit free

gravy la sauce [sohs]

gray gris [gree]

grease *(noun)* la graisse [grays]
(verb) graisser [gray-say]
greasy graisseux [gray-ser]

great grand [gron]
great! parfait! [pahr-fay]

green vert [vair]

greengrocer's un marchand de fruits et légumes [mahr-shon der frweez ay lay-goom]

grilled grillé [gree-yay]

grocer's une épicerie [aypees-ree]

ground: on the ground par terre [par tair]
on the ground floor au rez-de-chaussée [rayd-shoh-say]

group un groupe [groop]
our group leader notre chef [shef] de groupe
I'm with the American group je suis [jer swee] avec le groupe des Americains

guarantee une garantie [gahron-tee]

guest un invité [anvee-tay]
(in hotel) un client [klee-yon]
guesthouse une pension [pons-yon]

guide un guide [gheed]
a guidebook in English un guide en anglais [... ann on-glay]
guided tour une visite guidée [vee-zeet ghee-day]

guilty coupable [koo-pahbl]

guitar: do you play the guitar? est-ce que vous jouez de la guitare? [esker voo jway der lah ghee-tahr]

gums les gencives [jon-seev]

gun un revolver [rayvol-vair]
rifle un fusil [foo-zee]

gynecologist un gynécologue [jeenay-koh-log]

hair les cheveux [sher-ver]
  hairbrush une brosse à cheveux [bross . . .]
  haircut une coupe de cheveux [koop . . .]
  where can I get a haircut? où est-ce que je
  peux me faire couper les cheveux? [wesker jer
  per mer fair koo-pay lay sher-ver]
  is there a (ladies') hairdresser's here? est-ce
  qu'il y a un coiffeur (pour dames) ici?
  [. . . kwah-ferr poor dahm]
  hairdryer un sèche-cheveux [sesh sher-ver]
half la moitié [mwaht-yay]
  a half portion une demi-portion [der-mee
  pohrs-yon]
  half an hour une demi-heure [der-mee err]
ham du jambon [jon-bon]
hamburger un hamburger [onberr-gherr]
hammer un marteau [mahr-toh]
hand la main [man]
  handbag un sac à main
  handbrake le frein à main [fran . . .]
handkerchief un mouchoir [moo-shwahr]
handle la poignée [pwahn-yay]
hand luggage les bagages à main [bah-gahj ah
man]
handmade fait à la main [fay ay lah man]
handsome beau (belle) [boh, bel]
hanger un cintre [santr]
hangover la gueule de bois [gerl der bwah]
happen: what happened? qu'est-ce qui s'est
passé? [keskee say pah-say]
  I don't know how it happened je ne sais pas
  comment c'est arrivé [. . . koh-mon sayt
  ahree-vay]
  what's happening? qu'est-ce qui se passe?
  [keskee ser pass]
happy heureux [er-rer]
harbor le port [pohr]
hard dur [door]
  hard-boiled egg un oeuf dur [erf door]
  push hard poussez fort [. . . fohr]

harm: can it do (him) any harm? est-ce que ça peut (lui) faire du mal? [esker sah per lwee fair doo mal]

hat un chapeau [shah-poh]

hate: I hate... je déteste... [day-test]

have avoir [ah-vwahr]

   I have j'ai [jay]

   he/she has il/elle a [eel, el ah]

   we have nous avons [nooz ah-vōn]

   they have ils/elles ont [eelz ōn, elz ōn]

   do you have any cigars/a map? est-ce que vous avez des cigares/une carte? [esker vooz ah-vay...]

   can I have some water? est-ce que je peux avoir de l'eau? [esker jer per ah-vwahr...]

   I have to leave tomorrow je dois partir demain [jer dwah...]

   we have to... nous devons... [noo der-vōn]

hayfever le rhume des foins [room day fwān]

he il [eel]

head la tête [tait]

   headache un mal de tête [mal der tait]

   I have a (bad) headache j'ai (très) mal à la tête [jay tray mal...]

   headlights les phares [fahr]

   head waiter le maître d'hôtel [meitr-doh-tel]

   head wind un vent contraire [kōn-trair]

health la santé [sōn-tay]

   your health! à votre santé! [ah vohtr sōn-tay]

   healthy en bonne santé [ōn bon...]

hear entendre [ōn-tōndr]

   I can't hear je n'entends pas [jer nōn-tōn pah]

   hearing aid un appareil acoustique [ahpah-ray ahkoos-teek]

heart le coeur [kerr]

   heart attack une crise cardiaque [kreez kard-yak]

heat la chaleur [shal-lerr]

   heat stroke un coup de chaleur [koo der...]

heater un radiateur [rahd-yah-terr]

heating le chauffage [shoh-fahj]

central heating le chauffage central
[shoh-fahj sōn-trahl]
heavy lourd [loor]
heel le talon [tah-lōn]
  can you put new heels on these? est-ce que
vous pouvez me refaire les talons de ces
chaussures? [. . . mer rer-fair lay tah-lōn der
say shoh-soor]
height la hauteur [oh-terr]
  I'm 5 ft 6 je mesure un mètre soixante cinq
[jer mer-zoor ān maitr . . .]
hello bonjour [bōn-joor]
help aider [ay-day]
  can you help me? est-ce que vous pouvez
m'aider? [esker voo poo-vay may-day]
  can anybody help? est-ce que quelqu'un
[kel-kān] peut m'aider (or nous aider)?
  thanks for your help merci de votre aide
[mair-see der vohtr aid]
  help! au secours! [oh ser-koor]
her: I know her je la connais [. . . lah . . .]
  give her . . . donnez-lui . . . [. . . lwee]
  give it back to her rendez-le lui
  it's her c'est elle [sayt el]
  her bag see **his**
here ici [ee-see]
high haut [oh]
  high chair une chaise haute [shayz oht]
  higher up plus haut [ploo oh]
highway l'autoroute [ohtoh-root]
  » TRAVEL TIP: *toll highways in France (relatively
expensive); you either pay at the "péage" (toll-
station) or get a card there and pay on exit;
most highways are 2-lane only: be extra careful
where lanes merge; the Paris ring road ("le
périphérique") is toll-free*
hill une colline [koh-leen]
  (on road) une côte [koht]
him: I know him je le connais [. . . ler . . .]
  give him . . . donnez-lui . . . [. . . lwee]
  give it to him donnez-le lui

it's him c'est lui

his, her, its son [sōn], sa [sah], *(plural)* ses [say]

    it's his (her) bag, it's his (hers) c'est son sac,
c'est le sien [...ler see-yān]

    it's his (her) car, it's (his) hers c'est sa
voiture, c'est la sienne [...lah see-enn] *(in the
plural* les siens, les siennes)

hit: he hit me il m'a frappé [...frah-pay]

    the car hit him la voiture l'a heurté
[...err-tay]

hitch-hike faire de l'auto-stop [fair der
loh-toh-stop]

    hitch-hiker un auto-stoppeur [oh-toh
stoh-perr]

hold tenir [ter-neer]

    hold this tenez ça [ter-nay...]

    I'm holding it je le tiens [...tee-yān]

hole un trou [troo]

Holland la Hollande [oh-lōnd]

    in Holland en Hollande

home: at home chez moi [shay mwah]

    (back in America) chez nous [shay noo]

    I'm homesick j'ai le mal du pays [jay ler mal
doo pay-yee]

    we must go home nous devons rentrer

hommes men

honest honnête [oh-net]

    honestly? vraiment? [vray-mōn]

honey du miel [mee-yel]

honeymoon: our honeymoon notre lune de
miel [nohtr loon der mee-yel]

hood *(of car)* le capot [kah-poh]

hope: I hope that... j'espère que...
[jes-pair ker]

    I hope so/not j'espère que oui/non

horizon l'horizon [ohree-zōn]

horn *(car)* l'avertisseur [ahvair-tee-serr]

    I blew my horn j'ai klaxonné [jay
klaxoh-nay]

horrible horrible [oh-reebl]

hors d'oeuvre les hors d'oeuvre [ohr dervr]

horse un cheval [sher-val]
   horse-racing les courses de chevaux [koors der sher-voh]
hose un tuyau (souple) [twee-yoh soopl]
hospital un hôpital [ohpee-tal]
   will we have to go to the hospital? est-ce qu'il faut l'hospitaliser? [. . . lospee-tah-lee-zay]
host l'hôte [oht]
   hostess l'hôtesse [oh-tess]
hot chaud [shoh]
   (spiced) fort [fohr]
hotel un hôtel [oh-tel]
» *TRAVEL TIP: price is per room unless specified otherwise; breakfast extra; nominal charge for children sharing the room; prices must be displayed inside the room; there are plenty of inexpensive (one- and two-star) hotels in most towns; you may be asked to leave your passport at the reception desk when checking in*
hot plate une plaque chauffante [plak shoh-fōnt]
hot-water bottle une bouillotte [boo-yot]
hour une heure [err]
house une maison [may-zōn]
housewife une ménagère [maynah-jair]
how comment [koh-mōn]
   how are you?, how do you do? comment allez-vous? [koh-mōnt ah-lay voo]
   how many?, how much? combien [kōmb-yān]
   how much is it? combien ça coûte? [kōnb-yān sah koot]
   how many days? combien de jours?
   how long does it take to . . . ? combien de temps est-ce qu'il faut pour . . . ? [kōnb-yān der tōn eskeel foh poor]
   how long have you been here? vous êtes ici depuis combien de temps? [vooz ayt ee-see der-pwee kōnb-yān der tōn]
   how often do the buses run? il y a des bus tous les combien? [eelyah day boos too lay kōnb-yān]

how high/long/wide/deep is . . . ? quelle est la hauteur/longueur/largeur/profondeur de . . . ? [kel ay lah oh-ter, lōn-gher, lahr-jer, prohfōn-der der]

hull la coque [kok]

humid humide [oo-meed]

humor: you need a sense of humor il faut avoir le sens de l'humour [eel foht ah-vwahr ler sōns der loo-moor]

hungry: I'm hungry j'ai faim [jay fān]

I'm not hungry je n'ai pas faim [jer nay pah fān]

hurry: I'm in a hurry je suis pressé [jer swee pray-say]

please hurry! dépêchez-vous [daypay-shay-voo]

hurt blesser [blay-say]

I hurt myself je me suis fait mal [jer mer swee fay mal]

it hurts here ça fait mal ici [sah fay mal ee-see]

my leg/arm hurts j'ai mal à la jambe/au bras [jay mal ah . . .]

husband: my husband mon mari [mōn mah-ree]

I: I am je suis [jer swee]; **I have** j'ai [jay]

ice de la glace [glahs]

ice cream une glace

ice cream cone un cornet de glace [kor-nay . . .]

iced-coffee un café glacé [kah-fay glah-say]

with lots of ice avec beaucoup de glace [ah-vek boh-koo . . .]

ice-rink une patinoire [pahtee-nwahr]

identity papers les papiers d'identité [pahp-yay deedōn-tee-tay]

if si [see]

if we could si nous pouvions [see noo poov-yōn]

ignition l'allumage [ahloo-mahj]

ill malade [mah-lad]

I feel ill je ne me sens pas bien [jer ner mer
sŏn pah bee-yăn]
illegal illégal [eelay-gal]
illegible illisible [eelee-zeebl]
illness une maladie [mahlah-dee]
imitation-leather du simili-cuir [seemee-lee
kweer]
immediately tout de suite [toot sweet]
import importer [ănpohr-tay]
   import duty les droits d'importation [drwah
dănpohr-tahss-yŏn]
important: it's very important c'est très
important [say trayz ănpohr-tŏn]
impossible impossible [ănpoh-seebl]
impressive remarquable [rermahr-kahbl]
improve: I want to improve my French je
veux améliorer mon français [jer ver
ahmail-yoh-ray mŏn . . .]
in dans [dŏn]; **in France** en France [ŏn . . .]
   in New York à New York [ah . . .]
   in 1982 en 1982 [ŏn . . .]
   is he in? est-ce qu'il est là? [eskeelay lah]
inch un pouce [poos]
» *TRAVEL TIP: 1 inch = 2.54 cm*
include inclure [ăn-kloor]
   does that include breakfast? est-ce que le
petit-déjeuner est compris?
   is it included? est-ce que c'est compris dans
le prix?
   is everything included? est-ce que c'est tout
compris?
incompetent incompétent [ănkŏn-pay tŏn]
inconsiderate: he was inconsiderate il a
manqué d'égards [eel ah mŏn-kay day-gahr]
incontinent incontinent [ănkŏn-tee-nŏn]
incredible incroyable [ănkrwah-yahbl]
indecent indécent [ănday-sŏn]
independent indépendant [ănday-pŏn-dŏn]
India l'Inde [ănd]
indicator le clignotant [kleen-yoh-tŏn]
indigestion une indigestion [ăndee-jest-yŏn]

indoors à l'intérieur [ah lāntayr-yerr]
industry l'industrie [āndoos-tree]
infection une infection [ānfeks-yōn]
infectious contagieux [kōntahj-yer]
inflate gonfler [gōn-flay]
inflation l'inflation [ānflahs-yōn]
informal simple [sānpl]
   (not official) non-officiel [nonoh-fees-yel]
information: could you give me some
   information about ... ? est-ce que vous pouvez
   me renseigner sur [... rōnsayn-yay soor]
   do you have any information in English
   about ... ? est-ce que vous avez des
   informations en anglais sur ... ? [... dayz
   ānfohr-mahs-yōn ōnn ōn-glay soor]
   information office bureau de renseignements
   [boo-roh der rōnsayn-yer-mōn]
inhabitants les habitants [ahbee-tōn]
injection une piqûre [pee-koor]
injured: he's been injured il est blessé [eelay
   blay-say]
   badly injured gravement blessé
   [grahv-mōn ...]
injury une blessure [blay-soor]
innocent innocent [eenoh-sōn]
insect un insecte [ān-sekt]
   insect repellent une crème anti-insecte [krem
   ōn-tee ...]
inside à l'intérieur (de ...) [ah lāntair-yer der]
insist: I insist on it j'y tiens absolument [jee
   tee-yān apsoh-loo-mōn]
   I insist on ... je veux absolument ... [jer
   ver ...]
insomnia: I suffer from insomnia je souffre
   d'insomnie [jer soofr dānsom-nee]
instant coffee du café soluble [kay-fay soh-loobl]
instead à la place [ah lah plahs]
   instead of au lieu de [oh lee-yer der]
insulating tape de la bande isolante [bōnd
   eezoh lōnt]
insulation l'isolation [eezoh-lahs-yōn]

insult: he insulted me il m'a insulté [eel mah
ānsool-tay]

insurance une assurance [ahsoo-rōns]
  which is your insurance company? quelle
  est votre compagnie d'assurance?
  [. . . kōnpah-nee . . .]
  I'm insured je suis assuré [jer sweez
  ahsoo-ray]

intelligent intelligent [āntay-lee-jōn]

interdit *forbidden*
  interdit aux plétons *no pedestrians*

interesting: it's very interesting c'est très
  intéressant [say trayz āntay-ray-sōn]

international international [āntair-nahs-
  yoh-nal]

interpret: would you interpret for us? est-ce
  que vous pouvez nous servir d'interprète?
  [. . . noo sair-veer dāntair-pret]

intersection un croisement [krwahz-mōn]

into dans [dōn]

introduce: can I introduce . . . ? puis-je vous
  présenter . . . ? [pweej voo prayzōn-tay]

invalid un invalide [ānvah-leed]

invitation une invitation [ānvee-tahs-yōn]
  » *TRAVEL TIP: take a present such as flowers or a
  cake, but never a bottle of wine*

invite inviter [ānvee-tay]
  can I invite you out? puis-je vous inviter à
  sortir avec moi? [pweej vooz ānvee-tay ah sohr-
  teer ah-vek mwah]

invoice une facture [fak-toor]

Ireland l'Irlande [eer-lōnd]
  Irish irlandais [eerlōn-day]

iron *(clothes)* repasser [rerpah-say]
  (noun) un fer à repasser [fair ah . . .]

island une île [eel]

it: put it here mettez le (la) ici
  it is here il (elle) est ici
  where is it? *(a place, etc.)* où est-ce que c'est?
  [wesker say]; *(a particular object)* où est-ce
  qu'il (qu'elle) est? [weskeel ay]

give it to me donnez-le (la) moi
  it's him c'est lui [say . . .]
  it's not working ça ne marche pas [sah . . .]
Italy l'Italie [eetah-lee]
  Italian italien [eetahl-yān]
itch: it itches ça démange [sah day-mōnj]
itemize: would you itemize it for me? est-ce
  que vous pouvez me faire une facture détaillée
  [. . . fak-toor daytah-yay]
its *see* **his**
jack un cric [kreek]
jacket une veste [vest]
jam de la confiture [kōnfee-toor]
  traffic jam un embouteillage [ōnboo-tay-yahj]
January: in January en janvier [jōnv-yay]
jaw la mâchoire [mah-shwahr]
jealous jaloux [jah-loo]
jeans des jeans [djeenz]
jellyfish une méduse [may-dooz]
jetty la jetée [jer-tay]
jewelry des bijoux [bee-joo]
  jewelry store une bijourterie [beejoo-tree]
job un travail [trah-vie]
join: would you like to join us? est-ce que vous
  voulez venir avec nous? [. . . ver-neer ahvek
  noo]
joke une plaisanterie [playzōn-tree]
  you must be joking vous plaisantez! [voo
  playzōn-tay]
jours fériès *holidays*
  jour de fermeture *closed on . . .*
journey un voyage [voh-yahj]
July: in July en juillet [joo-yay]
June: in June en juin [jwān]
junk du bric à brac [breekah-brak]
just juste [joost]
  he's left just now il vient de partir [eel
  vee-yān der . . .]
  just there/a little juste là/un petit peu
  not just now pas pour l'instant [pah poor
  lāns-tōn]

that's just right ça va très bien [sah vah tray bee-yān]

keep: can I keep it? est-ce que je peux le garder? [. . . gahr-day]

keep the change gardez le monnaie [gahr-day lah moh-nay]

you didn't keep your promise vous n'avez pas tenu votre promesse [voo nah-vay pah ter-noo vohtr proh-mess]

it keeps on breaking ça se casse tout le temps [sahs kahs too ler tōn]

how long does it keep? combien de temps est-ce que ça se garde? [. . . sah ser gahrd]

ketchup *you will not find ketchup ("le ketchup")* [ket-sherp] *in a French restaurant, unless it's a fast-food establishment*

kettle une bouilloire [boo-ee-wahr]

key une clé [klay]

the key to room 7 please la clé de la chambre sept, s'il vous plaît

YOU MAY THEN HEAR . . .

je vous réveille à quelle heure? *when would you like to be wakened?*

kidneys les reins [rān]

(food) des rognons [rohn-yōn]

kill tuer [too-ay]

kilo un kilo [kee-loh]

» *TRAVEL TIP: conversion:* $\frac{kilos}{5} \times 11 = pounds$

kilos	1	1.5	2	3	5	10	20
lbs	2.2	3.3	4.4	6.6	11	22	44

kilometer un kilomètre [keeloh-maitr]

» *TRAVEL TIP: conversion: km ÷ 8 × 5 = miles*

kilometers	1	5	10	20	50	100
miles	0.62	3.11	6.2	12.4	31	62

kind: that's very kind of you c'est très aimable de votre part [say trayz ay-mahbl der vohtr par]

he's very kind il est très gentil [eel ay tray jōn-tee]

what kind of? quelle sorte de? [kel-sort-der]

kiss embrasser [ōnbrah-say]
  give me a kiss embrasse-moi [ōnbrahs mwah]
kitchen la cuisine [kwee-zeen]
knee le genou [jer-noo]
knife un couteau [koo-toh]
knitting needle une aiguille à tricoter [ay-gwee ah treekoh-tay]
knock: I knocked at the door j'ai frappé à la porte [frah-pay . . .]
  there's a knocking noise from the engine il y a le moteur qui cogne [eelyah ler moh-terr kee kon]
  he was knocked down by a car il a été renversé par une voiture [eel ah ay-tay rōnvair-say par oon vwah-toor]
knot un noeud [ner]
know savoir [sah-vwahr]
  I don't know je ne sais pas [jer ner say pah]
  I didn't know je ne savais pas [. . . sah-vay pah]
  we don't know nous ne savons pas [noo ner savōn . . .]
  I don't know him je ne le connais pas [. . . koh-nay pah]
  I don't know the area je ne connais pas la région
  do you know where/how? est-ce que vous savez où/comment? [esker voo say-vay oo, koh-mōn]
label une étiquette [aytee-ket]
laces des lacets [lay-say]
lacquer de la lacque [lak]
lady: the lady here told me . . . cette dame m'a dit . . . [set dam mah dee]
lake un lac
lamb *(meat)* de l'agneau [ahn-yoh]
lamp une lampe [lōnp]
  lampshade un abat-jour [ahbah-joor]
  lamppost un lampadaire [lōnpah-dair]
land *(verb)* atterrir [ahtay-reer]
  (noun) la terre [tair]

landscape le paysage [pay-ee-zahj]
lane une allée [ah-lay]
  (on highway, etc.) une voie [vwah]
  I was in the exit lane j'étais dans la voie de
  sortie [jay-tay dõn lah vwah der sohr-tee]
  the outside lane la voie de gauche [vwah der
  gohsh]
language une langue [lõng]
large grand [grõn]
laryngitis une laryngite [lahrãn-jeet]
last dernier [dairn-yay]
  last year/week l'année/la semaine dernière
  last night hier soir [yair swahr]
  (during the night) la nuit dernière [lah nwee
  dairn-yair]
  at last! enfin! [õnfãn]
late tard [tahr]
  sorry I'm late je m'excuse, je suis en retard
  [jer mex-kooz jer swee õn rer-tahr]
  later plus tard [ploo tahr]
  see you later à tout à l'heure [ah toot ah ler]
  at the latest au plus tard
laugh rire [reer]
laundrette une laverie automatique [lahv-ree
  ohtoh-mah-teek]
laundry detergent de la poudre à lessive [poodr
  ah lay-seev]
lavabos toilets
lawyer un avocat [ahvoh-kah]
laxative un laxatif [laxah-teef]
lazy paresseux [pahray-ser]
leader le chef [shef]
leaf une feuille [fer-ee]
leak une fuite [fweet]
  there's a leak in my ceiling il y a une fuite
  au plafond [. . . oh plah-fõn]
  gas leak une fuite de gaz
  the gas tank leaks le réservoir fuit [. . . fwee]
learn: I want to learn . . . je veux apprendre . . .
  [jer ver ah-prõndr]
lease *(verb)* louer [lway]; *(noun)* le bail [bie]

least: not in the least pas du tout [pah doo too]
    at least au moins [oh mwan]
    the least le moins
leather du cuir [kweer]
leave *(go away)* partir [pahr-teer]
    we're leaving tomorrow nous partons demain [pahr-ton . . .]
    when does the bus leave? quand est-ce que le bus part? [. . . pahr]
    we left Paris yesterday nous avons quitté Paris hier [nooz ah-von kee-tay . . .]
    I left two shirts in my room j'ai laissé deux chemises dans ma chambre [jay lay-say . . .]
    can I leave this here/with you? est-ce que je peux laisser ça ici/vous laisser ça? [esker jer per lay-say sah ee-see, voo lay-say sah]
left: on the left à gauche [ah gohsh]
    I'm left-handed je suis gaucher [jer swee goh-shay]
    left-luggage (office) la consigne [kon-seen]
leg la jambe [jonb]
legal: is it legal? est-ce que c'est légal? [. . . lay-gal]
lemon un citron [see-tron]
    lemonade de la limonade [leemoh-nad]
lend: will you lend me . . . ? est-ce que vous pouvez me prêter . . . ? [. . . pray-tay]
length la longueur [lon-gherr]
    lengthen rallonger [rahlon-jay]
lens *(of camera)* l'objectif [l'objek-teef]
Lent le Carême [kah-raim]
less: less expensive/far (than) moins cher/loin (que) [mwan . . . ker]
    less milk/money moins de lait/d'argent
lesson: French/skiing lessons des leçons de français/ski [ler-son . . .]
let: let me help laissez-moi vous aider [lay-say mwah vooz ay-day]
    let me/him go laissez-moi/le partir
    will you let me off here? laissez-moi descendre ici [. . . day-sondr ee-see]

let's go to allons à [ah-lōn ah]
let's go allons-y [ahlōnz-ee]
letter une lettre
are there any letters for me? est-ce qu'il y a du courrier pour moi? [. . . doo koor-yay poor mwah]
NB: *start a letter with "Monsieur" (or "Madame", "Mademoiselle") where you would have used "Dear Sir", etc, and with "Cher Monsieur" where you would have used "Dear Mr. Drew" etc. End the letter with "Veuillez agréer, Monsieur, l'expression de mes sentiments distingués", or with "Veuillez recevoir, cher Monsieur, l'expression de mes meilleurs sentiments" (less formal)*
lettuce une salade [sah-lad]
level: the oil level le niveau d'huile [nee-voh dweel]
liable responsable [respōn-sahbl]
librairie bookshop
library une bibliothèque [beeblee-oh-tek]
libre vacant; free
libre-service self-service
license un permis [pair-mee]
license plates les plaques d'immatriculation [plak deemah-tree-koo-lahs-yōn]
lid un couvercle [koo-vairkl]
lie un mensonge [mōn-sōnj]
can he lie down for a bit? est-ce qu'il peut s'étendre un moment [eskeel per say-tōndr ān momōn]
life la vie [vee]
lifeboat le canot de sauvetage [kah-noh . . .]
lifeguard le surveillant de plage [soorvay-yān der plahj]
life insurance une assurance-vie [ahsoo-rōns-vee]
life jacket le gilet de sauvetage [jee-lay . . .]
lift: do you want a lift? est-ce que je peux vous emmener quelque part? [. . . vooz ōnm-nay kel-ker pahr]

could you give me a lift (to Paris)? est-ce que vous pouvez m'emmener (jusqu'à Paris)? [... joos-kah ...]
light (not heavy) léger [lay-jay]
(not dark) clair [klair]
the lights aren't working *(house)* la lumière ne s'allume pas [lah loom-yair ner sah-loom pah]
(car) les phares ne s'allument pas [lay fahr ...]
have you got a light? est-ce que vous avez du feu? [esker vooz ah-vay doo fer]
can you turn the light on/off? est-ce que vous pouvez allumer/éteindre [ay-tāndr] la lumière?
when it gets light quand il fait jour [kōnt eel fay joor]
light bulb une ampoule [ōn-pool]
the bulb's gone out l'ampoule a sauté [ōn-pool ah sohtay]
a 100 watt bulb une ampoule de cent watts [... der sōn wat]
light meter le posemètre [pohz-maitr]
lighter un briquet [bree-kay]
like *(the same as)* comme [kom]
would you like ...? est-ce que vous voulez ...? [esker voo voo-lay]
I'd like coffee *etc.* j'aimerais un café *etc.* [jaym-ray ...]
I'd like to go j'aimerais partir
I like it ça me plaît [sah mer play]
I like you vous me plaisez [voo mer play-zay]
I don't like it ça ne me plaît pas
he doesn't like it ça ne lui plaît pas [... lwee play pah]
what's it like? c'est comment? [say koh-mōn]
do it like this faites comme ça [fayt kom sah]
one like that un comme ça [ān kom sah]
lime un citron vert [see-trōn vair]
line la ligne [leen]
(for tickets, etc.) une file d'attente [feel dah-tōnt]

lip la lèvre [laivr]
   lip salve de la pommade [poh-mad] pour les
   lèvres
   lipstick du rouge à lèvres [rooj ah laivr]
liqueur une liqueur [lee-kerr]
list une liste [leest]
   price list le tarif [tah-reef]
listen ècouter [aykoo-tay]
liter un litre [leetr]
» *TRAVEL TIP: 1 liter = 1.06 quarts = 0.22 gals*
   pints 0.44 0.87 1.75 3.50 5.25
   liters 0.25 0.5 1 2 3
little *(small)* petit [per-tee]
   a little un peu [ān per]
   a little ice un peu de glace
   a little more un peu plus [. . . ploo]
live[1]**: I live in America** j'habite en Amérique
[jah-beet ōnn ahmay-rik]
   where do you live? où est-ce que vous
   habitez? [wesker vooz ahbee-tay]
live[2] *(TV)* en direct [ōn dee-rekt]
   (wire, etc.) sous tension [soo tōns-yōn]
liver le foie [fwah]
   liver pate du pâté de foie
loaf un pain [pān]
lobster une langouste [lōn-goost]
local: a local wine un vin de la région [. . . der
lah rayj-yōn]
   a local restaurant un restaurant du coin
   [. . . doo kwān]
   it is made locally? est-ce que c'est fait ici?
   [esker say fay ee-see]
location de voitures car rental
lock: the lock's broken la serrure est abîmée
[lah say-roor ayt ahbee-may]
   it's locked c'est fermé à clé [fair-may ah klay]
   I've locked myself out/in je me suis enfermé
   dehors/dedans [jer mer swee ōnfair-may
   der-ohr, der-dōn]
   locker un casier [kahz-yay] (qui ferme à clé)
London Londres [lōndr]

lonely: I feel lonely je me sens seul [jer mer sōn serl]

long long [lōn]

will it take long? est-ce que ça va prendre longtemps? [... sah vah prōndr lōn-tōn]

we'd like to stay longer nous aimerions rester plus longtemps [nooz aymer-yōn res-tay ploo lōn-tōn]

that was long ago c'etait il y a longtemps [say-tay ele-yah...]

look: he looks ill/tired il a l'air malade/fatigué [eel ah lair...]

it looks unsafe ça a l'air dangereux [sah ah lair...]

it looks nice c'est joli [say...]

look at that regardez ça [rergahr-day sah]

can I look? est-ce que je peux regarder?

I'm just looking je regarde [jer rer-gahrd]

I'm looking forward to... je me réjouis de... [jer mer ray-jwee der]

I'm looking for... je cherche... [jer shairsh]

look out! attention! [ahtōns-yōn]

loose *(undone)* défait [day-fay]

lose perdre [pairdr]

I've lost my ... j'ai perdu mon (ma)... [jay pair-doo...]

I'm lost je me suis perdu [jer mer swee pair-doo]

lost and found le bureau des objets trouvés [boo-roh dayz ob-jay troo-vay]

lot: a lot (of) beaucoup (de) [boh-koo der]

not a lot pas beaucoup

a lot more expensive (than) beaucoup plus cher (que) [... ploo shair ker]

lotion une lotion [lohs-yōn]

loud fort [fohr]

speak louder parlez plus fort [pahr-lay ploo fohr]

*à **louer*** for rent

lounge le salon [sah-lōn]

love: I love you je vous aime [jer vooz aim]

he's in love (with) il est amoureux (de) [eel ayt ahmoo-rer]

I love this wine j'aime beaucoup ce vin [jaim boh-koo . . .]

lovely *(view, etc.)* très joli [tray joh-lee]
(dish, etc.) délicieux [daylees-yer]

we had a lovely vacation nous avons passé de merveilleuses vacances [nooz ah-von pah-say der mairvay-yerz vah-kons]

low bas [bah]

luck: good luck! bonne chance! [bon shons]

you're lucky vous avez de la chance [vooz ah-vay der lah shons]

that's lucky c'est de la chance

luggage les bagages [bah-gahj]

luggage rack le porte-bagages [port-bah-gahj]

lumbago un lumbago [lānbah-goh]

lump *(on body)* une grosseur [groh-serr]
(of sugar) un morceau [mohr-soh]

lunch le déjeuner [day-jer-nay]

YOU MAY SEE OR HEAR . . .

plat du jour [plah doo jour] *set menu*

» *TRAVEL TIP: the set menu is generally well worth trying; in Switzerland, "déjeuner" is commonly used for "breakfast"; use "dîner" for lunch*

lungs les poumons [poo-mon]

luxurious luxueux [looxoo-er]

luxury: a luxury hotel un hôtel de luxe [. . . der loox]

mad fou (folle) [foo, fol]

machine une machine [mah-sheen]

Madam Madame [mah-dam]

made-to-measure fait sur mesure [fay-soor mer-zoor]

magazine un magazine [mahgah-zeen]

magnificent magnifique [mahnee-feek]

maid la femme de chambre [fam der shonbr]

maiden name le nom de jeune fille [non der jern fee]

mail: can you mail this for me? est-ce que vous pouvez me poster ça? [. . . mer pos-tay sah]

....

is there any mail for me? est-ce qu'il y a du
courrier pour moi? [eskeel-yah doo koor-yay
poor mwah]
 mailbox une boîte aux lettres [bwaht oh laitr]
main principal [prān̄see-pal]
 the main roads les grandes routes [grōnd root]
make faire [fair]
 will we make it in time? est-ce qu'on y
 arrivera à temps [eskōnn ee ahreev-rah ah tōn]
 who is it made by? c'est fabriqué par qui?
 [say fahbree-kay par kee]
 makeup le maquillage [mahkee-yahj]
man un homme [om]
 the man at the desk said... le monsieur au
 guichet m'a dit... [ler mers-yer...]
manager: I would like to see the manager
 j'aimerais parler au directeur/la directrice
 [jem-ray par-lay oh deerek-terr/deerek-trees]
manicure: can I have a manicure? est-ce qu'on
 peut me faire les mains? [eskōn per mer fair
 lay mān̄]
many beaucoup [boh-koo]
 many places/people beaucoup d'endroits/de
 gens
map une carte [kart]
 a local map une carte de la région [...der la
 rayj-yōn]
 road map une carte routière [...root-yair]
 a map of Paris un plan de Paris [ān̄ plōn der
 pah-ree]
March: in March en mars [mahrs]
margarine de la margarine [mahrgah-reen]
marina un port de plaisance [pohr der play-zōns]
mark une marque [mahrk]
market un marché [mahr-shay]
 when is market day? quand est-ce que c'est
 jour de marché? [kōnt esker say joor der
 mahr-shay]
marmalade de la confiture d'oranges
 [kōnfee-toor doh-rōnj]
married marié [mahr-yay]

marry: we were married in 1960 nous nous
  sommes mariés en 1960 [noo noo som
  mahr-yay o͞n . . .]
   will you marry me? voulez-vous m'épouser?
   [voolay-voo maypoo-zay]
marvelous merveilleux [mairvay-yer]
mascara du mascara
mashed potatoes de la purée de pommes de
  terre [poo-ray der pom der tair]
mass *(in church)* la messe [mess]
massage un massage [mah-sahj]
mast mât [mah]
mat un petit tapis [per-tee tah-pee]
match: a box of matches une boîte
  d'allumettes [bwaht dahloo-met]
material *(cloth)* du tissu [tee-soo]
matter: it doesn't matter ça ne fait rien [sah
  ner fay ree-ya͞n]
   what's the matter? qu'est-ce qui ne va pas?
   [keskee ner vah pah]
mattress un matelas [mat-lah]
mature mûr [moor]
maximum le maximum [maxee-mom]
may: may I have/take . . . ? est-ce que je peux
  avoir/prendre . . . ? [esker jer per ah-vwahr,
  pro͞ndr]
   may we . . . ? est-ce que nous pouvons . . . ?
   [esker noo poo-vo͞n]
May: in May en mai [may]
maybe peut-être [pert-aitr]
mayonnaise de la mayonnaise [mah-yoh-nayz]
me: he knows me il me [mer] connaît
   he saw me il m'a vu
   give me . . . donnez-moi . . . [. . . mwah]
   give it to me donnez-le moi
   it's me c'est moi [say mwah]
meal un repas [rer-pah]
mean: what does this mean? qu'est-ce que ça
  veut dire? [kesker sah ver deer]
   by all means! bien entendu! [bee-ya͞nn
   o͞nto͞n-doo]

....

measles la rougeole [roo-johl]
   German measles la rubéole [roobay-ohl]
measure mesurer [merzoo-ray]
measurements les dimensions [deemōns-yōn]
meat de la viande [vee-yōnd]
mechanic: is there a mechanic here? est-ce
   qu'il y a un mécanicien ici? [eskeel-yah ān
   maykah-nees-yān ee-see]
medical: medical treatment un traitement
   [trait-mōn]
medicine *(drug)* un remède [rer-maid]
meet recontrer
   I met him last year je l'ai rencontré l'année
   dernière [jer lay rōnkōn-tray . . .]
   when shall we meet? quand est-ce que nous
   nous voyons? [kōntes-ker noo noo vwah-yōn]
   pleased to meet you enchanté(e) de faire
   votre connaissance [ōnshōn-tay der fair vohtr
   kohnay-sōns]
meeting une réunion [ray-oon-yōn]
melon un melon [mer-lōn]
member un membre [mōnmbr]
   how do I become a member? comment
   est-ce que je peux devenir membre? [koh-mōnt
   esker jer per derver-neer . . .]
memories les souvenirs
mend: can you mend this? est-ce que vous
   pouvez réparer ça? [. . . raypay-ray sah]
mention: don't mention it je vous en prie [jer
   vooz ōn pree]
menu: can I see the menu, please? est-ce que
   je peux voir la carte, s'il vous plaît? [esker jer
   per vwahr lah kart . . .]
   we'll have the set menu nous prenons le plat
   du jour [noo prer-nōn ler plah doo joor]
   do you have a set-price menu? est-ce que
   vous avez un menu touristique? [. . . mer-noo
   toorees-teek]
» *TRAVEL TIP: see the menu reader pp. 82–83*
mess: my room is a mess ma chambre est en
   désordre [. . . ōn day-zohrdr]

message: are there any messages for me?
est-ce qu'il y a une commission pour moi?
[eskeel-yah oon kohmees-yōn poor mwah]
can I leave a message for ...? est-ce que je
peux laisser un mot pour ...? [... lay-say ān
moh poor]
messieurs men
meter un mètre [maitr]
» *TRAVEL TIP: 1 meter = 39.37 ins = 1.09 yds*
feet   3.3 6.6 10 16.6 33 333
meters 1   2   3   5   10 100
meter un compteur [kōn-terr]
has the meter been read? est-ce qu'on a
relevé le compteur? [eskōnn ah rerl-vay ...]
métro subway
» *TRAVEL TIP: flat fare on whole network of Paris
métro; a "carnet de tickets" (book of 10 tickets)
is more economical than single tickets; tickets
valid on Paris bus network, but not on "RER"
(Greater Paris fast commuter train)*
midday midi [mee-dee]
at midday à midi
middle le milieu [meel-yer]
in the middle (of) au milieu (de)
midnight minuit [meen-wee]
at midnight à minuit
might: I might be late je serai peut-être en
retard [jer ser-ray pert-aitr ...]
I might come je viendrai peut-être [jer
vee-yān-dray pert-aitr]
he might have gone il est peut-être parti [eel
ay pert-aitr ...]
migraine une migraine [mee-grain]
mild doux [doo]
mile un mille [meel]
» *TRAVEL TIP: conversion: miles÷5×8=kilometers*
miles   0.5 1   3   5   10 50 100
kilometers 0.8 1.6 4.8 8   16 80 160
milk du lait [lay]
a glass of milk un verre de lait [vair der lay]
milkshake un milkshake

Entrées: Starters
Crudités *various salads and raw vegetables*
Terrine du chef *pâté maison*
Oeufs mayonnaise *eggs with mayonnaise*
Bouchées à la reine *chicken vol-au-vent*

Potages: Soups
Crème de bolets *cream of mushroom*
Velouté de tomates *cream of tomato*
Soupe à l'oignon *onion soup*

Viandes: Meat dishes
Boeuf *beef,* porc *pork,* veau *veal,* agneau *lamb*
Rôti de boeuf *roast beef*
Gigot d'agneau *roast leg of lamb*
Côtelette de porc *pork chop*
Foie de veau *veal liver*
Langue de boeuf *tongue*
Bifteck *steak*
Tournedos *fillet steak*
Escalope panée *slice of veal in breadcrumbs*
Paupiettes de veau *veal rolls*
Rognons madère *kidneys in madeira sauce*

Volaille: poultry
Poule au riz *chicken and rice*
Poulet rôti *roast chicken*
Canard à l'orange *duck with orange*

Chasse: game
Civet de lièvre *jugged hare*
Lapin chasseur *rabbit in white wine and herbs*

Poissons et marée: fish and seafood
Coquilles Saint-Jacques *scallops*
Huîtres *oysters*
Moules mariniére *mussels in white wine*
Truite aux amandes *trout with almonds*
Raie au beurre noir *skate in black butter*
Homard à l'armoricaine *lobster in white wine
sauce with shallots*
Cabillaud *cod,* langouste *crayfish,* langoustine
scampi, morue *salt cod*

A few menu terms: à l'ail *(with) garlic,* aux câpres *in caper sauce,* à la crème *with cream,* garni *with french fries (or rice) and vegetables,* en gelée *in aspic,* Provençale *cooked in olive oil with garlic, tomatoes and herbs,* au vin blanc *in white wine,* vinaigrette *sharp vinegar dressing*

Légumes: vegetables
Pommes de terre à l'anglaise *steamed potatoes,* pommes dauphine *potato croquettes,* (pommes) frites *french fries,* purée *mashed potatoes*
Chou *cabbage,* chou-fleur *cauliflower,* courgettes *zucchini,* épinards *spinach,* haricots verts *green beans,* petits pois *peas*

Salads
Salade *green salad with French dressing*
Salade niçoise *with green beans, peppers, anchovies, olives*
Salade russe *mixed vegetables in mayonnaise*

Fromages: le plateau de fromages *cheese board*

Dessert
Glace *ice cream,* flan *egg custard*
Tarte aux myrtilles *blueberry tart*
Cerises *cherries,* fraises *strawberries,* poire *pear,* pomme *apple,* pêche *peach,* raisin *grapes*

Snacks
Assiette anglaise *cold meats,* saucisse, frites *Frankfurter sausage and fries,* crêpes *pancakes,* croque-monsieur *toasted ham and cheese sandwich,* omelette au jambon/ fromage *ham/cheese omelette,* sandwich aux rillettes *potted meat sandwich*

Wines: *apart from the well-known "beaujolais" or more expensive "bourgogne" and "bordeaux", try "Côtes du Rhône" (red or white) and Anjou wines (rosé or white)* sec *dry,* demi-sac *medium dry*

Enjoy your meal!—or, as they say, **bon appétit!**

millimeter un millimètre [meelee-maitr]
minced meat de la viande hachée [vee-yōnd ah-shay]
mind: I've changed my mind j'ai changé d'avis [jay shōn-jay dah-vee]
  I don't mind ça ne me dérange pas [sahn mer day-rōnj pah]
  (it's all the same) ça m'est égal [sah mayt ay-gal]
  do you mind if I ... ? est-ce que ça vous dérange si ... ? [esker sah voo day-rōnj see]
  never mind tant pis [tōn pee]
mine *see* **my**
mineral water de l'eau minérale [oh meenay-rahl]
minimum le minimum [meenee-mom]
  the minimum charge le tarif minimum
minus moins [mwān]
minute une minute [mee-noot]
  in a minute dans un instant [dōnz ān āns-tōn]
  just a minute un instant
mirror une glace [glahs]
  (rear view) le rétroviseur [raytroh-vee-zerr]
Miss Mademoiselle [mahd-mwah-zel]
miss: we missed the train/boat nous avons manqué le train/bateau [nooz ah-vōn mōn-kay ...]
  I miss you vous me manquez [voo mer mōn-kay]
  my wallet/sister is missing mon portefeuille/ma soeur a disparu [... ah deespah-roo]
  there's something/there are 2 people missing il y a quelque chose qui manque/deux personnes qui manquent [eelyah kelker-shohz ... kee mōnk]
mist la brume [broom]
mistake une erreur [ay-rerr]
  I think you've made a mistake je crois que vous vous êtes trompé [jer krwah ker voo vooz ait trōn-pay]

**misunderstanding: there's been a misunder-
standing** il y a eu un malentendu [eelyah oo
ān mahlōn-tōn-doo]

mix mélanger [maylōn-jay]

modern moderne [moh-dairn]

moisturizer une lotion hydratante [lohs-yōn
eedrah-tōnt]

moment un moment [moh-mōn]

Monday lundi [lān-dee]

money: I've lost my money j'ai perdu mon
argent [jay pair-doo mōn ahr-jōn]

I have no money je n'ai pas d'argent [jer nay
pah dahr-jōn]

» *TRAVEL TIP: French currency*
*The unit is "un franc", divided up into 100
"centimes"; main coins are 10 centimes, 20c,
50c, 1F, 2F, 5F and 10F; the 10F coin is easily
mistaken for other large coins; main notes are
10F, 20F, 50F 100F, 500F*

month un mois [mwah]

monument un monument [mohnoo-mōn]

moon la lune [loon]

moorings *(ropes)* les amarres [ah-mahr]

moped un cyclomoteur [seekloh-moh-terr]

more plus [ploo(s)]

more expensive (than) plus cher (que) [ploo
shair ker]

more people/money plus de gens/d'argent
[ploos der . . .]

can I have some more? est-ce que je peux en
avoir plus? [. . . ōnn ah-vwahr ploos]

more wine, please encore du vin, s'il vous
plaît [ōn-kor doo vān . . .]

no more, thank you merci, ça suffit [mair-see
sah soo-fee]

no more money plus [ploo] d'argent

I haven't got any more je n'en ai plus [jer
nōnn ay ploo]

there aren't any more il n'y en a plus [eeln
yōnn ah ploo]

morning le matin [mah-tān]

in the morning le matin
in the following morning le lendemain matin [lōnd-mān mah-tān]
mosquito un moustique [moos-teek]
most: the most... le plus... [ler ploo]
I like this one the most c'est celui-ci que je préfère [say ser-lwee-see ker jer pray-fair]
most of the people la plupart du temps/des gens [lah ploo-par doo tōn, day jōn]
that's most kind c'est très gentil [say tray jōn-tee]
motel un motel [moh-tel]
mother: my mother ma mère [mair]
motor le moteur [moh-ter]
motorbike une moto [moh-toh]
motorboat un canot automobile [kah-noh ohtoh-moh-beel]
motorcyclist un motocycliste [mohtoh-see-kleest]
motorist un automobiliste [ohtoh-moh-bee-leest]
mountain une montagne [mōn-tan]
in the mountains à la montagne
mountaineering l'alpinisme [alpee-neesm]
mouse une souris [soo-ree]
moustache une moustache [moos-tahsh]
mouth la bouche [boosh]
move bouger [boo-jay]
don't move ne bougez pas [ner boo-jay pah]
could you move your car? est-ce que vous pouvez déplacer votre voiture? [... dayplah-say vohtr vwah-toor]
movie le film [fēlm]
movie theater un cinéma [seenay-mah]
» *TRAVEL TIP: tip the usher; no smoking*
Mr. Monsieur, M.
Mrs. Madame [mah-dam], Mme
Ms *no equivalent in French*
much beaucoup [boh-koo]
much better/much more beaucoup mieux/plus
not much pas beaucoup [pah...]
muffler le silencieux [selōns-yer]

mug: I've been mugged j'ai été attaqué [ahtah-kay]
   coffee mug une grande tasse [grōnd tahs]
muscle un muscle [mooskl]
   I've strained a muscle je me suis claqué un muscle [jer mer swee klah-kay ...]
museum un musée [moo-zay]
» TRAVEL TIP: *most museums and castles are closed on Tuesdays in France*
mushroom un champignon [shōnpeen-yōn]
music la musique [moo-zeek]
mussels des moules [mool]
must devoir [der-vwahr]
   I must go je dois partir [jer dwah ...]
   we must not... nous ne devons pas ... [noo ner der-vōn pah]
   you must... vous devez ... [voo der-vay]
mustard de la moutarde
mutton du mouton [moo-tōn]
my mon [mōn], ma [mah], *(plural)* mes [may]
   it's my bag/it's mine c'est mon sac, c'est le mien [... ler mee-yān]
   it's my car, it's mine c'est ma voiture, c'est la mienne [... lah mee-yen] *(plural:* "les miens, les miennes")
nail *(on finger)* un ongle [ōngl]
   (in wood, etc.) un clou [kloo]
   nail clippers une pince à ongles [pāns ...]
   nail file une lime à ongles [leem ...]
   nail polish du vernis à ongles [vair-nee ...]
   nail scissors des ciseaux à ongles [see-zoh ...]
naked nu [noo]
name un nom [nōn]
   first name le prénom [pray-nōn]
   my names is... je m'appelle ... [jer mah-pel]
   what's your name? quel est votre nom? [kel-ay vohtr nōn]
   what's the name of...? comment s'appelle ...? [koh-mōn sah-pel]
napkin une serviette [sairv-yet]

narrow étroit [ay-trwah]
national national [nahs-yoh-nal]
nationality la nationalité [nahs-yoh-nah-lee-tay]
natural naturel [nahtoo-rel]
naughty: don't be naughty soyez sage
[swah-yay sahj]
near: is it near? est-ce que c'est près [esker say
pray]
  near here/home près d'ici/de chez nous [pray
dee-see, der shay noo]
  where's the nearest pharmacy/bank? où est
la pharmacie/banque la plus proche? [oo ay . . .
lah ploo prosh]
  do you go near . . . ? est-ce que vous passez
près de . . . ? [. . . pah-say pray der]
  nearly presque [presk]
neat *(drink)* sec
necessary nécessaire [naysay-sair]
neck le cou [koo]
necklace le collier [kol-yay]
need: I need a . . . j'ai besoin d'un . . . [jay
ber-zwān]
  he needs . . . il a besoin de . . .
  I/we need to leave je dois/nous devons partir
[jer dwah, noo der-vōn . . .]
needle une aiguille [ay-gwee]
negative *(photo)* un négatif [naygay-teef]
neighbor un voisin [vwah-zān]
neither: neither of them aucun des deux
[oh-kān day der]
  neither I nor . . . ni moi ni . . . [nee mwah nee]
  neither do I moi non plus [mwah nōn ploo]
nephew: my nephew mon neveu [ner-ver]
nervous nerveux [nair-ver]
net: net price le prix net [pree net]
nettoyage à sec dry cleaning
never jamais [jah-may]
  I've never been there je n'y suis jamais allé
[jer nee swee jah-mah ah-lay]
new nouveau [noo-voh]
  (not used) neuf [nerf]

news les nouvelles [noo-vel]
    newspaper un journal [joor-nal]
    do you have any English newspapers? est-ce que vous avez des journaux anglais? [. . . day joor-noh ōn-glay]
    newsstand un kiosque à journaux [kee-yosk ah joor-noh]
New Year la nouvelle année [noo-vel ah-nay]
    on New Year's day le jour de l'An [ler joor der lōn]
  » *TRAVEL TIP: usually an occasion for a big meal with friends, "le réveillion" [rayvay-yōn]*
    on New Year's Eve à la Saint Sylvestre [ah lah sān seel-vaistr]
    happy New Year bonne année [bon ah-nay]
New Zealand la Nouvelle Zélande [noo-vel zay-lōnd]
next *(bus, train)* prochain [pro-shān]
    next to . . . à côté de . . . [ah koh-tay der]
    stop at the next corner arrètez-vous au prochain croisement [ahray-tay voo oh proh-shān krwahz-mōn]
    see you next year! à l'année prochaine! [ah lay-nay proh-shān]
    next week la semaine prochaine [lah ser-main proh-shān]
    when is the next train? quand part le prochain train? [kōn par ler proh-shān . . .]
    where is the next stop? où est le prochain arrêt? [oo ay ler proh-shain ah-ray]
nice *(nice-looking)* joli [joh-lee]
    (pleasant, kind) gentil [jōn-tee]
niece: my niece ma nièce [nee-yes]
night la nuit [nwee]
    at night la nuit
    nightclub un night-club
    nightgown une chemise de nuit [sher-meez . . .]
    night porter le portier de nuit [pohrt-yay . . .]
no *(reply)* non [nōn]
    there's no water/toilet paper il n'y a pas d'eau/de papier hygiénique [eelnyah pah der . . .]

I have no money je n'ai pas d'argent [jer nay pah . . .]
nobody personne [pair-son]
  nobody saw him personne ne l'a vu [pair-son ner . . .]
noise le bruit [brwee]
  it's very noisy il y a beaucoup de bruit
  our room is too noisy notre chambre est trop bruyante [nohtr shōnbr ay troh brwee-yōnt]
none aucun [oh-kān]
  none of them aucun d'entre eux [. . . dōntr er]
nonsense: I don't want any nonsense je ne veux pas d'histoires [jern ver pah dees-twahr]
nonsmoker non-fumeurs [nōn foo-mer]
noon: at noon à midi [mee-dee]
normal normal [nohr-mal]
north le nord [nor]
North America l'Amérique du Nord [ahmay-reek doo nor]
Northern Ireland l'Irlande du Nord [eer-lōnd doo nor]
nose le nez [nay]
  I have a nosebleed je saigne du nez [jer sayn . . .]
not pas [pah]
  not me/that one pas moi/celui-là
  I'm not hungry je n'ai pas faim [jer nay pah . . .]
  he's not here il n'est pas là [eel nay pah . . .]
  I don't want . . . je ne veux pas . . . [jer ner ver pah]
  he doesn't understand il ne comprend pas [eel ner . . . pah]
  I didn't . . . je n'ai pas . . .
  he didn't tell me il ne m'a pas dit
  there isn't any . . . il n'y a pas de . . .
notepaper du papier à lettres [pahp-yay ah laitr]
nothing rien [ree-yān]
  there's nothing il n'y a rien
notice: I didn't notice (that) . . . je n'ai pas remarqué (que) . . . [jer nay pah rermahr-kay ker]

November: in November en novembre
[noh-vōnbr]
now maintenant [mānt-nōn]
nowhere nulle part [nool par]
nudist un nudiste [noo-deest]
   nudist beach une plage réservée aux
   nudistes
nuisance: it's a nuisance ce'st ennuyeux [sayt
   ōn-nwee-yer]
   he's being a nuisance il nous importune [eel
   nooz ānpor-toon]
numb engourdi [ōngoor-dee]
number le numéro [noomay-roh]
   (quantity) le nombre [nōnbr]
nurse une infirmière [ānfeerm-yair]
nut *(for bolt)* un écrou [ay-kroo]
   (to eat) no single general term; be specific
   see **peanuts**
nylon du nylon [nee-lon]
oar une rame [rahm]
objets trouvés *lost property*
obligatory obligatoire [ohblee-gah-twahr]
obvious: it's obvious c'est évident [set
   ayvee-dōn]
occasionally de temps en temps [der tōnz ōn
   tōn]
occupied occupé [ohkoo-pay]
   is this seat occupied? est-ce que cette place
   est prise? [. . . set plass ay preez]
o'clock *see* **time**
October: in October en octobre [ōnn ok-tohbr]
octopus un poulpe [poolp]
odd *(strange)* bizarre
   odd number un nombre impair [nōnbr ān-pair]
odometer le compteur kilométrique [kōn-terr
   keeloh-may-treek]
off: 10% off dix pour cent de réduction [dee poor
   sōn der raydooks-yōn]
   it came off c'est tombé [say tōn-bay]
   can you switch it off? est-ce que vous pouvez
   l'éteindre? [. . . ay-tāndr]

offense un délit [day-lee]
offensive injurieux [ān̄joor-yer]
offer: can I offer you...? puis-je vous
offrir...? [pweej vooz oh-freer]
office un bureau [boo-roh]
officer *(to policeman)* Monsieur l'agent
[mers-yer lah-jōn̄]
official officiel [ohfees-yel]
(person) un employé [ōn̄plwah-yay]
often souvent [soo-vōn̄]
oil de l'huile [weel]
(cooking) de l'huile comestible [kohmes-teebl]
(petroleum) du pétrole [pay-trol]
I'm losing oil je perds [pair] de l'huile
will you change the oil? est-ce que vous
pouvez me faire une vidange? [... mer fair oon
vee-dōn̄j]
ointment une pommade [poh-mad]
O.K. d'accord [dah-kor]
it's O.K. ça va [sah vah]
old vieux (vieille) [vee-yer, vee-yay]
how old are you? quel âge avez-vous? [kel ahj
ah-vay voo]
olive une olive [oh-leev]
green/black olives des olives vertes/noires
[... vairt, nwahr]
omelette une omelette
cheese/ham omelette une omelette au
fromage/jambon [ohm-let oh froh-mahj, jōn̄-bōn̄]
on sur [soor]
I haven't got it on me je ne l'ai pas sur moi
[jer ner lay pah soor mwah]
turn the light on allumez la lumière
[ahloo-may...]
on Monday, etc. lundi, etc.
on Mondays, etc. le lundi, etc.
on television à la télévision
once une fois [oon fwah]
at once tout de suite [toot sweet]
one un (une) [ān̄, oon]
the red one le (la) rouge

one-way street une rue à sens unique [roo ah sōns oo-neek]

one-way: I'd like a one-way ticket to j'aimerais un billet aller pour [... bee-yay ah-lay ...]

onion un oignon [ohn-yōn]

only seulement [serl-mōn]

open ouvert [oo-vair]

when do you open? quand est-ce que vous ouvrez? [kōnt esker vooz oo-vray]

I can't open it je n'arrive pas à l'ouvrir [jer nah-reev pah ah loo-vreer]

open return un billet de retour "open" [bee-yay der rer-toor ...]

opera un opéra [ohpay-rah]

opera house l'opéra

operation une opération [ohpay-rahs-yōn]

will I need an operation? est-ce qu'il faudra m'opérer? [eskeel foh-drah mohpay-ray]

operator *(telephone)* l'opératrice [ohpay-rah-trees]

» *TRAVEL TIP: dial 10 to call the operator, and 12 (renseignements) for international calls and inquiries*

opposite en face (de) [ōn fahs der]

optician un opticien [optees-yān]

or ou [oo]

orange une orange [oh-rōnj]

orange juice un jus [joo] d'orange

orchestra un orchestre [ohr-kestr]

order: could we order now? est-ce qu'on peut commander maintenant? [eskōn per kohmōn-day mānt-nōn]

thank you, we've already ordered merci, nous avons déjà commandé

it's out of order ça ne marche pas [sah ner marsh pah]

original original [ohree-jee-nal]

other autre [ohtr]

the other one l'autre

do you have any others? est-ce que vous en avez d'autres?

otherwise autrement [ohtrer-mon]
ought: I ought to go je devrais partir [jer der-vray par-teer]
ounce *1 ounce = 28.35 grams*
our notre [nohtr], nos [noh]
  our car/son notre voiture/fils
  our tickets/cars nos billets/voitures
  it's ours c'est le (la) nôtre [ler, lah nohtr]
  these are ours ce sont les nôtres [lay nohtr]
out dehors [der-ohr]
  we're out of gas nous n'avons plus d'essence [noo nah-von ploo . . .]
outboard un hors-bord [ohr-bohr]
outdoors dehors [der-ohr]
outlet *(electrical)* une prise de courant [preez der koo-ron]
outside dehors [der-ohr]
  can we sit outside? est-ce qu'on peut se mettre dehors?
ouvert *open*
over: over here ici [ee-see]
  over there là-bas [lah-bah]
  he's over 40 il a plus de [ploo der] quarante ans
  it's all over c'est fini [say fee-nee]
overboard: man overboard! un homme à la mer! [ann om ah lah mair]
overcharge: you've overcharged me la facture est trop élevée [lah fak-toor ay trohp ayl-vay]
overcooked trop cuit [troh kwee]
overexposed surexposé [soorex-poh-zay]
overnight la nuit [nwee]
  we want to stay overnight nous voulons passer la nuit ici [. . . pah-say la nwee . . .]
oversleep: I overslept j'ai dormi trop longtemps [jay dor-mee troh lon-ton]
overtake dépasser [daypah-say]
owe: what do I/we owe you? combien est-ce que je vous dois/nous vous devons? [konb-yan esker jer voo dwah, noo voo der-von]
  you owe me 10F vous me devez dix francs [voo mer der-vay]

own: my own... mon propre... [prohpr]
  I'm on my own je suis seul [jer swee serl]
owner le propriétaire [prohpree-yay-tair]
oxygen l'oxygène [oxee-jen]
oysters des huîtres [weetr]
pack: I haven't packed yet je n'ai pas encore
  fait mes bagages [jer nay pahz ōn-kot fay may
  bah-gahj]
packet: a packet of... un paquet de...
  [pah-kay]
padlock un verrou [vay-roo]
page la page [pahj]
  could you page him? est-ce que vous pouvez
  le faire appeler? [...ler fair ap-lay]
pain: I've got a pain here j'ai mal ici [jay mal
  ee-see]
  I've got a pain in my leg/back j'ai mal à la
  jambe/aux reins
  painkillers des calmants [kal-mōn]
painful douloureux [dooloo-rer]
painting un tableau [tah-bloh]
pair: pair of gloves/shoes une paire de
  gants/chaussures [pair der...]
pajamas pyjamas [peejah-mah]
pale pâle [pahl]
pancake une crêpe [kraip]
panties un slip
pants *(trousers)* un pantalon [pōntah-lōn]
paper *(newspaper)* un journal [joor-nal]
  a piece of paper un (morceau de) papier
  [mohr-soh der pahp-yay]
  paper tissues des mouchoirs en papier
  [moo-shwahr...]
parcel un colis [koh-lee]
pardon *(I didn't understand)* pardon...
  [pahr-dōn]
  I beg your pardon *(sorry)* excusez-moi
  [eskoo-zay mwah]
parents: my parents mes parents [pah-rōn]
Paris Paris [pah-ree]
park *(noun)* un parc

where can I park my car? où est-ce que je peux garer ma voiture? [wesker jer per gah-ray mah vwah-toor]
parking lot un parking
» *TRAVEL TIP: zoned parking in most towns: you must display a "disque de stationnement" (parking permit) on your windshield; for further information go to the local "syndicat d'initiative" (tourist office)*
part: part of une partie de [pahr-tee der]
  (spare) part une pièce de rechange [pee-yes der rer-shōnj]
partner *(business)* un associé [ahsohs-yay]
  (games) un partenaire [parter-nair]
party *(group)* un groupe [groop]
  (celebration) une réunion [ray-oon-yōn]
  (in the evening) une soirée [swah-ray]
  I'm with the American party je suis avec le groupe americain
pass *(mountain)* un col
  he's passed out il s'est évanoui [eel sayt ayvah-nwee]
passable *(road)* praticable [prah-tee-kahbl]
passage souterrain underground walkway
  passage protégé stretch of main road where traffic coming from the side roads doesn't have right of way
passenger un passager [pahsah-jay]
passerby un passant [pah-sōn]
passport: my passport mon passeport [pass-pohr]
past: in the past autrefois [ohtr-fwah]
  do you go past the station? est-ce que vous passez devant la gare? [esker voo pah-say der-vōn . . .]
pasta des pâtes [paht]
pastry de la pâtisserie [pahtees-ree]
path un chemin [sher-mān]
patient: be patient soyez patient [swah-yay pahs-yōn]
pâtisserie bakery

pattern *(design)* un dessin [day-sãn]
pay *(verb)* payer [pay-yay]
  can I pay, please? est-ce que je peux payer,
  s'il vous plaît?
PCV: communication en PCV collect call
pea: peas des petits pois [per-tee pwah]
peace la paix [pay]
peach une pêche [pesh]
péage toll
peanuts: salted peanuts des cacahuètes salées
  [kahkah-wet sah-lay]
pear une poire [pwahr]
pebble un galet [gah-lay]
pedal la pédale [pay-dahl]
pedestrian un piéton [pee-yay-tõn]
  pedestrian crossing un passage pour piétons
  [pah-sahj . . .]
» *TRAVEL TIP: do not assume that cars will stop or*
  even slow down once you are on a pedestrian
  crossing; be extra cautious, especially with
  children
peg *(for tent)* un piquet de tente [pee-kay der
  tõnt]
  (clothes) une pince à linge [pãns ah lãnj]
pelvis le bassin [bah-sãn]
pen: have you got a pen? est-ce que vous avez
  un stylo? [. . . stee-loh]
pencil un crayon [kray-yõn]
penpal un correspondant [kohres-põn-dõn]
penicillin la pénicilline [paynee-see-leen]
penknife un canif [kah-neef]
pension guesthouse
pensioner un retraité [rertray-tay]
people les gens [jõn]
  how many people? combien de personnes?
  [pair-son]
pepper du poivre [pwahvr]
  green/red peppers des poivrons verts/rouges
  [pwah-vrõn vair, rooj]
peppermint une pastille de menthe [pahs-tee
  der mõnt]

....

per: percent pour cent [poor sōn]
   per day/week/person par jour
   /semaine/personne
perfect parfait [par-fay]
   the perfect vacation des vacances idéales
   [vah-kōns eeday-ahl]
performance *(theater, etc.)* une représentation
   [rerpray-zōn-tahs-yōn]
perfume un parfum [pahr-fān]
perhaps peut-être [per-taitr]
périphérique *le périphérique is the Paris ring road*
period *(menstruation)* les règles [raygl]
   (time) une période [payr-yod]
perm une permanente [pairmah-nōnt]
permanent permanent [pairmah-nōn]
permit un permis [pair-mee]
permission une permission [pairmees-yōn]
person une personne [pair-son]
   in person en personne
personal personnel [pairsoh-nel]
   for personal use à usage personnel
   I'd like to make a personal call j'aimerais
   une communication avec préavis
   [. . . kohmoo-nee-kahs-yōn ah-vek pray-ah-vee]
pet un animal domestique [ahnee-mal
   dohmes-teek]
pharmacy une pharmacie [fahrmah-see]
phone *see* **telephone**
photograph une photo
   would you take a photograph of us? est-ce
   que vous pouvez nous prendre en photo? [esker
   voo poo-vay noo prōndr ōn fohtoh]
piano un piano
pickpocket un pickpocket
picture *(photo)* une photo
picnic un pique-nique [peek-neek]
piece: a piece of . . . un morceau de . . .
   [mohr-soh]
piétons *pedestrians*
pig un cochon [koh-shōn]
pigeon un pigeon [pee-jōn]

pile-up une collision en chaîne [kohleez-yōn . . .]
pill: do you take the pill? est-ce que vous prenez
la pilule? [esker voo prer-nay lah pee-lool]
pillow un oreiller [ohray-yay]
pin une épingle [ay-pāngl]
pineapple un ananas [ahnah-nas]
pink rose [rohz]
pint = *approx.* un demi-liter [dermee-leetr]
» *TRAVEL TIP: 1 pint = 0.57 liter; if you ask for a*
beer, the standard measure is 0.33 l, slightly
more than a half-pint (0.26 l)
pipe un pipe [peep]
(for water) un tuyau [twee-yoh]
pipe tobacco du tabac [tah-bah] pour la pipe
piston un piston [pees-tōn]
pity: it's a pity! c'est dommage! [doh-mahj]
place: is this place taken? est-ce que cette
place [plahs] est prise?
do you know any good places to go? est-ce
que vous connaissez des endroits [an-drwah]
intéressants?
places debout *standing room*
places assises *seated accommodation*
plain simple [sānpl]
plain omelette une omelette nature
[. . . nah-toor]
plain fabric du tissu uni [. . . oo-nee]
plan: we plan to . . . nous avons l'intention
de . . . [nooz ah-vōn lāntōns-yōn der]
plane un avion [ahv-yōn]
plant *(flower, etc.)* une plante [plōnt]
(factory) une usine [oo-zeen]
plaster *(cast)* un plâtre [plahtr]
plastic: plastic bag un sac en plastique [sak ōn
plahs-teek]
plate une assiette [ahs-yet]
platform: which platform? quel quai? [kel kay]
play jouer [joo-ay]
somewhere for the children to play un
endroit où les enfants peuvent jouer [ānn
ōn-drwah oo layz ōnfōn perv joo-ay]

pleasant agréable [ahgray-ahbl]
please s'il vous plaît [seel voo play]
  could you please...? s'il vous plaît,
  est-ce que vous pouvez...? [...esker voo
  poo-vay]
  yes, please oui, s'il vous plaît
  I am pleased to/with... je suis content
  de... [jer swee kōn-tōn der]
pleasure: it's a pleasure bien volontiers
  [bee-yān vohlōnt-yay]
  with pleasure avec plaisir [ah-vek play-zeer]
plenty: plenty of... beaucoup de... [boh-koo
  der]
  thank you, that's plenty merci, ça suffit
  [...sah soo-fee]
pliers des tenailles [ter-nah-ee]
plug *(electrical)* une prise [preez]
  (sink, etc.) la bonde [bōnd]
plum une prune [proon]
plumber un plombier [plōnb-yay]
  plumbing la plomberie [plōn-bree]
plus plus [ploos]
p.m.: 1 p.m. une heure de l'après-midi [oon err
  der lay-pray-mee-dee]
  7 p.m. sept heures du soir [set err doo swahr]
pneumonia une pneumonie [pnermoh-nee]
poached egg un oeuf poché [erf poh-shay]
pocket une poche [posh]
poids lourds *freight trucks*
point: could you point to it? est-ce que vous
  pouvez me l'indiquer? [...āndee-kay]
  four point six quatre virgule six
  [...veer-gool...]
  points *(car)* les vis platinées [vees
  plahtee-nay]
police la police [poh-lees]
  get the police! appelez la police! [ap-lay...]
  policeman un agent de police [ah-jōn der
  poh-lees]
  police station le commissariat
  [kohmee-sahr-yah]

YOU MAY SEE...

gendarmerie *police station (the "gendarmes" operate outside large cities and on the roads)*

polish *(for shoes)* du cirage [see-rahj]

could you polish my shoes? est-ce que vous pouvez cirer mes souliers? [...see-ray may sool-yay]

polite poli [poh-lee]

politics la politique

polluted pollué [pohloo-ay]

pool *(swimming)* une piscine [pee-seen]

poor pauvre [pohvr]

(quality) médiocre [maid-yohkr]

popular populaire [pohpoo-lair]

is it popular? *(place)* est-ce que c'est très fréquenté? [esker say tray fraykōn-tay]

population la population [pohpoo-lahs-yōn]

pork du porc [pohr]

port *(harbor)* un port [pohr]

(drink) du porto

to port à bâbord [ah bah-bohr]

porter un porteur [por-terr]

portrait un portrait [por-tray]

posh chic

possible possible [poh-seebl]

could you possibly...? est-ce que vous pourriez...? [esker voo poor-yay]

postcard une carte postale [...pohs-tahl]

post office la poste

general delivery la poste restante [pohst res-tōnt]

» *TRAVEL TIP: you can telephone from any post office (open 8 a.m. to 7 p.m. and 8–12 Sat. mornings); in Paris the main post office is open 24 hrs. a day, 7 days a week: 52 rue du Louvre; mail boxes are yellow; you may be asked to show your passport when collecting general delivery items*

YOU MAY SEE...

colis *parcels*

timbres *stamps*

....

poster un poster [pos-tair]
postman le facteur [fak-terr]
potato une pomme de terre [pom der tair]
  potato chips des chips [cheeps]
pottery une poterie [pot-ree]
pound une livre [leevr]; *NB: the "livre" is 500g*
  » *TRAVEL TIP: conversion: pounds÷11×5=kilos*

pounds	1	3	5	6	7	8	9
kilos	0.4	1.4	2.3	2.7	3.2	3.6	4.1

poussez push
pour verser [vair-say]
  it's pouring il pleut à verse [eel pler ah vairs]
powder la poudre [poodr]
  powdered milk du lait en poudre
power outage une panne d'électricité [pan
  daylek-tree-see-tay]
prawns des crevettes roses [krer-vet rohz]
  prawn cocktail un cocktail de crevettes
prefer: I prefer . . . je préfère . . . [jer pray-fair]
pregnant: she is pregnant elle est enceinte
  [el ayt ōn-sānt]
prepare préparer [praypah-ray]
prescription: can you make up this prescription?
  est-ce que vous pouvez préparer cette
  ordonnance? [. . . praypah-ray set ohrdoh-nōns]
present: at present à présent [ah pray-zōn]
  here's a present for . . . voilà un cadeau
  pour . . . [vwahla ān kah-doh poor]
  it's for a present c'est pour offrir [say poor
  oh-freer]
president le président [prayzee-dōn]
press: could you press these? est-ce que vous
  pouvez repasser ces vêtements? [rerpah-say say
  vait-mōn]
pressing dry cleaning
pressure la pression [prays-yōn]
prêt-à-porter ready-to-wear
pretty joli [joh-lee]
  pretty expensive assez cher [ah-say . . .]
price le prix [pree]
  price list le tarif [tah-reef]

prière de... *please...*
priest un prêtre [praitr]
primeurs *early produce*
print *(photo)* une épreuve sur papier [ay-prerv soor pahp-yay]
  one print of each une épreuve de chaque [...shahk]
printed matter des imprimés [ānpree-may]
priorité (à droite) *right of way (to vehicles coming from the right)*
prison une prison [pree-zōn]
private: private beach/road plage/route privée [...pree-vay]
probably probablement [prohbab-bler-mōn]
problem un problème [proh-blem]
product un produit [proh-dwee]
profit un bénéfice [baynay-fees]
program un programme
  (on radio, TV) une émission [aymees-yōn]
promise: I promise that... je promets que... [jer proh-may ker]
pronounce: how do you pronounce that? comment est-ce que ça se prononce? [koh-mōnt esker sah ser proh-nōns]
propeller une hélice [ay-lees]
properly correctement [kohrek-ter-mōn]
property: it's my property ça m'appartient [sah mahpart-yān]
propriété privée *private, no trespassing*
protect protéger [prohtay-jay]
Protestant protestant [prohtes-tōn]
proud fier [fee-yair]
prove: I can prove it je peux le prouver [jer per ler proo-vay]
PTT *Post Office*
public: the public le public [poo-bleek]
public holidays les jours fériés [joor fayr-yay]
» *TRAVEL TIP: public holidays: Jan. 1st; Easter; May 1st; Ascension Day; July 14th ("fete nationale"); Aug. 15th ("l'Assomption"); Nov. 1st ("la Toussaint"); Nov. 11th (Remembrance Day); Dec. 25th*

pull *(verb)* tirer [tee-ray]
  he pulled out in front of me il a déboîté juste devant moi [eel ah daybwah-tay joost der-vōn mwah]
pump une pompe [pōnp]
punctual ponctuel [pōnktoo-el]
puncture: I've had a puncture j'ai eu une crevaison [. . . krervay-zōn]
pure pur [poor]
purple violet [vee-yoh-let]
purpose: on purpose exprès [ex-pray]
purse un porte-monnaie [port-moh-nay]
push pousser [poo-say]
put: where can I put . . . ? où est-ce que je peux mettre . . . ? [wesker jer per maitr]
  where have you put it? où est-ce que vous l'avez mis? [wesker voo lah-vay mee]
quai at station: platform
quality la qualité [kahlee-tay]
quarantine: to stay in quarantine rester en quarantine [. . . kahrōn-ten]
quarter: a quarter of an hour un quart d'heure [kahr-der]
question une question [kest-yōn]
quick rapide [rah-peed]
  that was quick c'était vite fait [say-tay veet fay]
  quickly rapidement [rahpeed-mōn]
quiet tranquille [trōn-keel]
  be quiet! ne faites pas de bruit [ner fait pah der brwee]
quite *(fairly)* assez [ah-say]; *(very)* très [tray]
race une course [koors]
radiator un radiateur [rahd-yah-terr]
radio: on the radio à la radio [rahd-yoh]
rail: by rail en train [ōn trān]
rain la pluie [plwee]
  it's raining il pleut [pler]
  raincoat un imperméable [ānpair-may-ahbl]
ralentir slow down
rally *(car)* un rallye [rah-lee]

rape: I've been raped on m'a violée [ōn mah vee-yoh-lay]

rappel *on traffic signs: reminder*

rare rare [rahr]

  (steak) saignant [sayn-yōn]

rarely rarement [rahr-mōn]

rash une éruption de boutons [ayroops-yōn der boo-tōn]

raspberries des framboises [frōn-bwahz]

rat un rat [rah]

rate: do you have a special rate for children/students? est-ce que vous avez un tarif réduit pour les enfants/étudiants? [. . . ān tah-reef ray-dwee . . .]

  what's the exchange rate for dollars? quel est le taux du dollar?

rather *(fairly)* assez [ah-say]

  I'd rather je préférerais [pray-fair-ray]

raw cru [kroo]

razor un rasoir [rah-zwahr]

  razor blades des lames de rasoir [lahm . . .]

read: something to read quelque chose à lire [kel-ker shohz ah leer]

  would you read this for me? est-ce que vous pouvez me lire ça? [. . . mer leer sah]

ready: when will it be ready? ce sera prêt quand? [ser serah pray kōn]

  I'm not ready yet je ne suis pas encore prêt [jer ner swee pahz ōn-kor pray]

real *(leather, etc.)* véritable [vayree-tahbl]

  really? vraiment? [vray-mōn]

rear-view mirror le rétroviseur [raytroh-vee-zerr]

reasonable raisonnable [rayzoh-nahbl]

receipt: can I have a receipt? est-ce que je peux avoir une quittance? [. . . kee-tōns]

receive recevoir [rerser-vwahr]

recently récemment [raysah-mōn]

reception *(hotel)* la réception [rayseps-yōn]

  at a reception à la réception

receptionist la réceptionniste [rayseps-yoh-neest]

recipe une recette [rer-set]
recommend: can you recommend...?
 est-ce que vous pouvez recommander...?
 [...rerkoh-mon-day]
record *(music)* un disque [deesk]
red rouge [rooj]
reduction une réduction [raydooks-yon]
refill une recharge [rer-shahrj]
refrigerator un frigo [free-goh]
refuse: I refuse... je refuse... [jer rer-fooz]
region: in this region dans cette région
 [don set rayj-yon]
**registered: I'd like to send this registered
 mail** j'aimerais envoyer ça en recommandé
 [jaym-ray onvwah-yay sah on rerkoh-mon-day]
remain rester [res-tay]
remember: do you remember? est-ce que vous
 vous rappelez? [esker voo voo rap-lay]
  I don't remember je ne me rappelle pas [jer
  ner mer rah-pel pah]
renseignements *inquiries*
rent: can I rent a car/bicycle? est-ce que je peux
 louer une voiture/bicyclette? [esker jer per loo-ay...]
 YOU MAY HEAR...
 une taxe kilométrique [tax keeloh-may-treek]
 = *mileage charge*
repair: can you repair it? est-ce que vous
 pouvez le réparer? [...ler raypah-ray]
repeat: could you repeat that slowly? est-ce
 que vous pouvez répéter lentement?
 [...raypay-tay lont-mon]
replace *(give another)* remplacer [ronplah-say]
reply une réponse [ray-pons]
R.E.R. [air-er-air] *fast commuter train in the
 Greater Paris area*
rescue sauver [soh-vay]
reservation une réservation [rayzair-vahs-yon]
reserve réserver [rayzair-vay]
  can I reserve a seat? est-ce que je peux
  réserver une place? [esker jer per rayzair vay
  oon plahs]

we have reserved a table for 2 nous avons réservé une table pour deux [noo zahvon rayzair-vay oon tahbl poor der]

responsible responsable [respon-sahbl]

rest: the rest of le reste de [rest]

I've come here for a rest je suis venu ici pour me reposer [. . . mer rerpoh-zay]

rest rooms: where are the rest rooms? où sont les toilettes? see also **toilet**

public rest rooms des toilettes [twah-let] publiques

» TRAVEL TIP: public toilets are sometimes scarce and difficult to find; remember that cafés and bars always provide such facilities

restaurant un restaurant [restoh-ron]

» TRAVEL TIP: it often pays to look for a place off the main road; see the menu reader, pp. 82–83

retail price le prix de détail [pree der day-tah-ee]

retired: I am retired je suis à la retraite [jer sweez ah lah rer-trait]

return retourner [rertoor-nay]

reverse gear la marche arrière [marsh ahr-yair]

rez-de-chaussée ground floor

rheumatism des rhumatismes [roomah-teesm]

rib une côte [koht]

rice du riz [ree]

rich riche [reesh]

ridiculous ridicule [reedee-kool]

riding: I'd like to go riding j'aimerais faire du cheval [jaym-ray fair doo sher-val]

right: that's right c'est juste [say joost]

you're right vous avez raison [vooz ah-vay ray-zon]

on the right à droite [ah drwaht]

ring *(on finger)* une bague [bag]

ripe *(fruit)* mûr [moor]

river une rivière [reev-yair]

(main river) un fleuve [flerv]

road une route [root]

which is the road to . . . ? quelle est la route
pour . . . ?

rob: I've been robbed on m'a dévalisé [ōn mah
dayvah-lee-zay]

rock *(stone)* un rocher [roh-shay]

on the rocks avec de la glace [ah-vek der lah
glahs]

roll *(bread) the closest equivalent would be:* un
petit pain [per-tee pān]

Roman Catholic catholique [kahtoh-leek]

romantic romantique [rohmōn-teek]

roof le toit [twah]

roof rack la galerie [gal-ree]

room: there isn't enough room il n'y a pas
assez de place [eeln-yah pahz ah-say der plahs]

have you got a single/double room? est-ce
que vous avez une chambre pour une
personne/deux personnes? [. . . oon shōnbr poor
oon pair-son . . .]

for one night/two nights pour une nuit/deux
nuits [poor oon nwee, der nwee]

YOU MAY THEN HEAR . . .

c'est complet [say kōn-play] *sorry, we're full*

avec douche [doosh] *with shower*

avec cabinet de toilette [kahbee-nay der
twah-let] *with private toilet*

avec salle de bain [sahl der bān] *with private
bathroom*

room number le numéro de la chambre
[noomay-roh . . .]

room service le service des chambres
[sair-vees . . .]

rope une corde [kord]

rose une rose [rohz]

rosé: a bottle of rosé une bouteille de rosé
[boo-tay der roh-zay]

rough: the sea is rough la mer est mauvaise
[lah mair ay moh-vayz]

roughly approximativement
[ahproxee-mah-teev-mōn]

round *(circular)* rond [rōn]

round trip un voyage aller et retour [. . . ah-lay ay rer-toor]

roundtrip: a roundtrip/two roundtrips to . . . un/deux aller retour pour . . . [. . . ahlay rer-toor poor]

roundabout un rond-point [ron-pwan]

» *TRAVEL TIP: let cars coming from the right go first, even when you are on the roundabout*

route un itinéraire [eetee-nay-rair]

which is the prettiest/fastest route? quel est l'itinéraire le plus agréable/rapide?

» *TRAVEL TIP: travel planning will be easier with the yellow Michelin road maps (1 cm = 2 km); secondary roads are generally good, and a sensible alternative to highways*

routiers *"relais routiers" are good inexpensive restaurants catering primarily for truck drivers; don't hesitate to try them (look for a red and blue circular sign)*

row boat une barque [bark]

rubber du caoutchouc [kah-oo-tshoo]

rubber band en élastique [aylass-teek]

rubbish les ordures [ohr-door]

when is rubbish collected? quand est-ce qu'il y a le ramassage des ordures [kont eskeel yah le rahmah-sahj . . .]

it's rubbish ça ne vaut rien [sahn voh ree-yan]

rudder le gouvernail [goovair-nah-ee]

rude impoli [anpoh-lee]

rum du rhum [rom]

run courir [koo-reer]

(engine) marcher [mahr-shay]

hurry, run! vite, dépêchez-vous! [veet daypay-shay-voo]

I've run out of gas/money je n'ai plus d'essence/d'argent [jer nay ploo day-sons, dahr-jon]

he ran into my car il est rentré dans ma voiture [eel ay ron-tray don . . .]

sables mouvants *quicksand*

sad triste [treest]

....

safe sans danger [sōn dōn-jay]
  will it be safe here? est-ce que ça ne risque
  rien ici? [. . . reesk ree-yān ee-see]
  is it safe to swim here? est-ce qu'on peut se
  baigner sans danger, ici? [eskōn per ser
  bayn-yay sōn dōn-jay . . .]
safety sécurité [saykoo-ree-tay]
  safety pin épingle de sureté [ay-pāngl der
  soor-tay]
sail une voile [vwahl]
  can we go sailing? est-ce qu'on peut faire de
  la voile? [eskōn per fair . . .]
» *TRAVEL TIP: check weather conditions at the
  "capitainerie" (harbor master's office)*
  sailor un marin [mah-rān]
salad une salade [sah-lad]
sale: is it for sale? est-ce qu'on peut l'acheter?
  [eskōn per lash-tay]
salesclerk un vendeur (une vendeuse) [vōn-derr,
  vōnderz]
salle à manger dining room
salle d'attente waiting room
salmon le saumon [soh-mōn]
salt le sel
same le (la) même [maim]
  the same again, please la même chose, s'il
  vous plaît [lah maim shohz . . .]
  the same to you à vous pareillement [ah voo
  pahray-ee-mōn]
  it's all the same to me ça m'est égal [sah
  mait ay-gal]
sample *(a wine, etc.)* goûter [goo-tay]
  (of product) un échantillion [ayshōn-tee-yōn]
sand le sable [sahbl]
sandals des sandales [sōn-dahl]
sandwich un sandwich
  ham/cheese sandwich sandwich au
  jambon/fromage [. . . oh jōn-bōn, froh-mahj]
» *TRAVEL TIP: not made with square sliced bread;
  usually a section of French baguette sliced
  lengthways*

sanitary napkin une serviette hygiénique [sairv-yet eej-yay-neek]

sans issue dead end

satisfactory satisfaisant [sahtees-fer-zoṅ]

Saturday samedi [sam-dee]

sauce la sauce [sohz]

  saucepan une casserole [kas-rohl]

saucer ne soucoupe [soo-koop]

sauna un sauna [soh-nah]

sausage un saucisse [soh-sees]

  (cold) un saucisson [sohsee-soṅ]

save *(life)* sauver [soh-vay]

say: how do you say in French...? comment est-ce qu'on dit en français...? [koh-moṅt eskoṅ dee oṅ froṅ-say]

  what did he say? qu'est-ce qu'il a dit? [kes-keel ah dee]

scarf un foulard [foo-lar]

scenery le paysage [payee-zahj]

schedule *(timetable)* un horaire [oh-rair]

  (program) un programme

  on schedule à l'heure [ah lerr]

  behind schedule en retard [rer-tahr]

  scheduled flight un vol régulier [vol raygool-yay]

school une école [ay-kol]

scissors une paire de ciseaux [pair der see-zoh]

Scotland l'Écosse [ay-kos]

  Scottish écossais [aykoh-say]

scrambled eggs des oeufs brouillés [er broo-yay]

scratch une éraflure [ayrah-floor]

scream: I heard somebody scream j'ai entendu quelqu'un crier [...kree-yay]

screw une vis [vees]

  screwdriver un tournevis [toorner-vees]

sea la mer [mair]

  by the sea au bord de la mer [oh bor der...]

seafood des fruits de mer [frweed mair]

seafront le bord de mer [bor der mair]

search chercher [shair-shay]

search party une expédition de secours [expay-dees-yōn der ser-koor]

seasick: I get/feel seasick j'ai le mal de mer [jay ler mal der mair]

seaside le bord de la mer [bor der lah mair]

season une saison [say-zōn]

high/low season haute/basse saison [oht, bahs . . .]

season ticket une carte d'abonnement [kart dahbon-mōn]

seasoning l'assaisonnement [ahsay-zon-mōn]

seat *(in train, etc.)* une place [plahs]
(chair, etc.) un siège [see-yayj]

is this somebody's seat? est-ce que cette place est occupée? [esker set plahs ayt ohkoo-pay]

seat belt une ceinture de sécurité [sān-toor der saykoo-ree-tay]

» *TRAVEL TIP: wearing of seat belts compulsory outside towns*

I'd like a window seat/a seat facing the engine j'aimerais une place près de la fenêtre/dans le sens de la marche [. . . pray der lah fer-naitr, dōn ler sōns der lah marsh]

seaweed des algues [alg]

second une seconde [ser-gōnd]
(2nd) deuxième [derz-yem] *(date)* le deux [der]

secondhand d'occasion [dohkahz-yōn]

secretary une secrétaire [serkray-tair]

sedative un calmant [kal-mōn]

see: I see je vois [vwah]

can I see the room? est-ce que je peux voir la chambre? [. . . vwahr . . .]

have you seen . . . ? est-ce que vous avez vu? [. . . voo]

see you à bientôt [ah bee-yān-toh]

see you tonight/tomorrow à ce soir/demain [ah ser swahr, der-mān]

seem: it seems that . . . il semble que . . . [eel sōnbl ker]

self: self-service self-service [. . . sair-vees]

self-contained indépendant [ā͞nday-pō͞n-dō͞n]

sell vendre [vō͞ndr]

send envoyer [ō͞nvwah-yay]

sens unique one-way

sensitive sensible [sō͞n-seebl]

separate[1] séparer [saypah-ray]

    I'm separated je suis séparé de ma femme [jer swee saypah-ray der mah fam]

    (woman) je suis séparée de mon mari [. . . der mō͞n mah-ree]

separate[2] séparé

    can we pay separately? est-ce qu'on peut payer chacun pour soi? [eskō͞n per pay-yay shah-kā͞n poor swah]

September: in September en septembre [sep-tō͞nbr]

serious sérieux [sair-yer]

    is it serious? *(injury, etc.)* est-ce que c'est grave? [. . . grahv]

serrez à droite keep to the right

serum *(for snake bite)* du sérum [say-rom]

serve: are you serving breakfast now? est-ce que vous servez le petit-déjeuner maintenant? [. . . sair-vay . . .]

service le service [sair-vees]

    is the service charge included? est-ce que le service est compris?

service station une station-service [stahs-yō͞n sair-vees]

set *(fix)* fixer [fee-xay]

    (adjust) régler [ray-glay]

several plusieurs [plooz-yerr]

sew coudre [koodr]

shade: in the shade à l'ombre [ah lō͞nbr]

shake secouer [serkoo-ay]

» *TRAVEL TIP: shaking hands ("se serrer la main") is common on meeting and leaving somebody*

shallow peu profond [per proh-fō͞n]

shame: it's a shame c'est dommage [doh-mahj]

shampoo un shampooing [shō͞n-pwā͞n]

shampoo and set une mise en plis [meez on plee]

shape la forme [form]

share partager [pahrtah-jay]

sharp *(blade, etc.)* coupant [koo-pon]

shave: I must shave je dois me raser [. . . mer rah-zay]

 shaving cream de la mousse à raser [moos ah rah-zay]

she elle [el]

sheep un mouton [moo-ton]

sheet un drap [drah]

 (paper) une feuille de papier [fer-ee der pahp-yay]

shelf une étagère [aytah-jair]

shell *(egg, nut)* la coquille [koh-kee]

 (sea) un coquillage [kohkee-yahj]

 shellfish des coquillages

shelter un abri [ah-bree]

sherry un xérès [gzay-res]

shin le tibia [teeb-yah]

ship un bateau [bah-toh]

shirt une chemise [sher-meez]

 see **chest, collar**

shock un choc [shok]

 I got an electric shock from j'ai reçu une décharge électrique de [jay rer-soo oon day-sharj aylek-treek]

 shock absorber un amortisseur [ahmor-tee-serr]

shoes des chaussures [shoh-soor]

» *TRAVEL TIP: shoes sizes*

US	4	5	6	7	8	9	10	11
Continent	37	38	39	41	42	43	44	46

shop un magasin [mahgah-zan]

shopping: I have some shopping to do j'ai des courses à faire [jay day koors ah fair]

» *TRAVEL TIP: opening hours: food shops usually 7:30 to 12:30 and 3:30 to 7:30; other shops 9 to 12 and 2 to 7; closing day gen. Mon. (or half day Mon.); bakers and small grocers often open on Sun. morning*

shore: on the shore sur le rivage [... ree-vahj]

short court [koor]

    I'm 3 short il m'en manque trois [eel mōn mōnk ...]

    short cut un raccourci [rahkoor-see]

shorts un short

shoulder l'epaule [ay-pohl]

shout crier [kree-yay]

show *(exhibition)* une exposition [expoh-zees-yōn]

    (theater, etc.) un spectacle [spek-tahkl]

    please show me montrez-moi, s'il vous plaît [mōn-tray mwah ...]

shower une douche [doosh]

shrimps des crevettes grises [krer-vet greez]

shrink: does it shrink? est-ce que ça rétrécit? [esker sah raytray-see]

shut fermer [fair-may]

    shut up! taisez-vous! [tay-zay-voo]

shy timide [tee-meed]

sick malade [mah-lad]

    I feel sick je ne me sens pas bien [jer ner mer sōn pah bee-yān]

    he's been sick il a vomi [eel ah voh-mee]

side le côté

    on this side de ce côté

    on the other side de l'autre côté

    side street une rue de traverse [roo der trah-vairs]

    by the side of the road au bord de la route [oh bor der lah root]

sidewalk le trottoir [troh-twahr]

sight: out of sight hors de vue [or der voo]

    the sights of ... les choses à voir dans ... [lay shohz ah vwahr ...]

    we'd like to go on a sight-seeing tour nous voudrions faire une visite guidée [noo voodree-yōn fair oon vee-zet ghee-day]

sign *(road)* un panneau [pah-noh]

    (notice) un écriteau [aykree-toh]

signal: he didn't signal il n'a pas mis son clignotant [... mee sōn kleen-yoh-tōn]

signature une signature [seen-yah-toor]
silk la soie [swah]
silly stupide [stoo-peed]
silver: a silver chain une chaînette en argent
  [. . . ōnn ahr-jōn]
similar semblable [sōn-blahbl]
simple simple [sānpl]
since: since last week depuis la semaine
  dernière [der-pwee . . .]
  since we arrived depuis notre arrivée
  since you want. . . puisque vous voulez . . .
  [pwees-ker . . .]
sincerely *see* **letter**
sing chanter [shōn-tay]
single: single room une chambre pour une
  personne [shōnbr poor oon pair-son]
  I'm single je suis célibataire [jer swee
  saylee-bah-tair]
sink un lavabo [lahvah-boh]
  (boat) couler [koo-lay]
  (kitchen) l'évier [ayv-yay]
Sir. . . Monsieur . . . [mers-yer]
  see **letter**
sister: my sister ma soeur [serr]
sit: can I sit here est-ce que je peux m'asseoir
  ici [. . . ah-swahr . . .]
  sit next to me asseyez-vous à côté de moi
  [ahsay-yay voo . . .]
size la taille [tie]
  (of shoes) la pointure [pwān-toor]
  do you have my size? est-ce que vous avez
  ma taille/pointure? [esker vooz ah-vay . . .]
  YOU MAY HEAR OR SEE . . .
  petit [per-tee] *small*
  moyen [mwah-yān] *medium*
  grand [grōn] *large*
skates des patins [pah-tān]
  skating rink une patinoire [pahtee-nwahr]
skis des skis [skee]
  ski boots des chaussures de ski [shoh-soor . . .]
  ski poles des bâtons de ski [bah-tōn . . .]

ski lift un remonte-pente [rer-mont-pont]
ski run une piste [peest]
skid déraper [dayrah-pay]
skin la peau [poh]
skin-diving la plongée sous-marine [plon-jay
soo-mah-reen]
skirt une jupe [joop]
sky le ciel [see-yel]
sled une luge [looj]
sleep: I can't sleep je ne peux pas dormir
[. . . dor-meer]
  sleeper *(train)* un wagon-lit [vah-gon-lee]
  sleeping bag un sac de couchage [sak der
  koo-shahj]
  sleeping pills des somnifères [somnee-fair]
sleeve une manche [monsh]
slice une tranche [tronsh]
slides *(photographic)* des diapositives
[dee-yah-poh-zee-teev]
slippery glissant [glee-son]
slow lent [lon]
  could you speak a little slower? est-ce que
  vous pouvez parler un peu plus lentement?
  [. . . an per ploo lont-mon]
small petit [per-tee]
  small change de la petite monnaie [per-teet
  moh-nay]
smallpox la variole [vahr-yohl]
smell: there's a funny smell il y a une odeur
  bizarre [eelyah oon oh-derr . . .]
  it smells ça sent [sah son]
smoke la fumée [foo-may]
  do you smoke? est-ce que vous fumez? [esker
  voo foo-may]
  can I smoke est-ce que je peux fumer?
» *TRAVEL TIP: smoking is prohibited in France in
  public buildings and on public transport, as
  well as in movie theaters*
snack un casse-croûte [kahs-kroot]
snake un serpent [sair-pon]
S.N.C.F. the French Railways

snorkel un tuba [too-bah]
snow la neige [nej]
   powder snow la neige poudreuse
   [. . . poo-drerz]
so: it's so hot that . . . il fait si chaud que . . .
   [eel fay see shoh ker]
   not so much pas tant [pah-tōn]
   so so comme çi comme ça [komsee-komsah]
soaked: we are soaked nous sommes trempés
   [noo som trōn-pay]
soap un savon [sah-vōn]
socks une paire de chaussettes [pair der shoh-set]
soda water de l'eau [oh] de seltz
soft doux [doo]
   soft drinks des boissons san alcool [bwah-sōn
   sōnz al-kol]
soldes sale
sole *(fish)* une sole
   (shoe) une semelle [ser-mel]
   could you put new soles on these? est-ce
   que vous pouvez ressemeler ces chaussures?
   [. . . rers-mer-lay say shoh-soor]
some: some places certains endroits
   [sair-tān . . .]
   can I have some? est-ce que je peux en avoir?
   [esker jer per ōnn ah-vwahr]
   some bread du [doo] pain; **some beer** de la
   [der lah] bière; **some potato chips** des [day]
   chips
   can I have some more? est-ce que je peux en
   avoir plus? [. . . ōnn ah-vwahr ploos]
somebody quelqu'un [kel-kān]
something quelque chose [kel-ker shohz]
sometimes quelquefois [kelker-fwah]
somewhere quelque part [kel-ker par]
son: my son mon fils [fees]
song une chanson [shōn-sōn]
sonnez please ring
soon bientôt [bee-yān-toh]
   as soon as possible dès que possible [day ker
   poh-seebl]

sooner plus tôt [ploo toh]
sore: it's sore ça fait mal [sah fay mal]
   I have a sore throat j'ai mal à la gorge [jay
   mal ah lah gohrj]
sorry: I'm sorry excusez-moi [exkoo-zay-mwah]
sort: will you sort the problem out? est-ce que
   vous pouvez arranger ça? [...ahrōn-jay sah]
sortie de camions *truck crossing*
sortie de secours *emergency exit*
sound: it sounds interesting ça a l'air
   intéressant [sah ah lair...]
soup une soupe [soop]
sour aigre [aigr]
sous-sol *basement*
south le sud [sood]
   South Africa l'Afrique de Sud [ah-freek...]
souvenir un souvenir [soov-neer]
spade *(for beach)* une pelle [pel]
Spain l'Espagne [es-pan]
   in Spain en Espagne [ōnn...]
   Spanish espagnol [espan-yol]
spare: spare parts des pièces de rechange
   [pee-yes der rer-shōnj]
   spare tire la roue de secours [roo der ser-koor]
spark plugs les bougies [boo-jee]
speak: do you speak English? est-ce que vous
   parlez anglais? [esker voo par-lay ōn-glay]
   is there somebody who speaks English?
   est-ce qu'il y a quelqu'un qui parle anglais?
   [...kel-kān kee parl ōn-glay]
   I don't speak French je ne parle pas français
   [jer ner parl pah frōn-say]
special spécial [spays-yal]
specialist un spécialiste [spays-yah-leest]
specially spécialement [spays-yal-mōn]
speed la vitesse [vee-tes]
   he was speeding il allait trop vite [eel ah-lay
   troh veet]
   speed limit une limitation de vitesse
   [leemee-tahs-yōn...]
   speedometer le compteur de vitesse [kōn-terr]

» *TRAVEL TIP: speed limit: in towns 60 km/h (38 mph); on roads 90 km/h (56 mph); on two-lane highways 110 km/h (70 mph); on highways 130 km/h (81 mph)*

spell: how do you spell it? comment ça s'écrit [koh-mōn sah say-kree]

spend *(money)* dépenser

(time) passer

spices des condiments [kōndee-mōn]

is it spicy? est-ce que c'est très épicé?
[. . . aypee-say]

spider une araignée [ahrain-yay]

spirits des spiritueux [spee-ree-too-er]

spoon une cuillère [kwee-yair]

sprain une entorse [ōn-tohrs]

I've sprained my ankle je me suis foulé la cheville [jer mer swee foo-lay . . .]

spring *(season)* le printemps [prān-tōn]

(metal) un ressort [rer-sor]

(water) une source [soors]

square *(in town)* une place [plahs]

2 square meters deux mètres carrés
[. . . maitr kah-ray]

staff le personnel [pairsoh-nel]

stairs les escaliers [eskahl-yay]

stalls: 2 stalls deux orchestre [derz or-kestr]

stamp: 2 stamps for America deux timbres [tānbr] pour Amérique

book of stamps carnet de timbres [karnay der tānbr]

what's the postage for . . . ? il faut affranchir à combien pour . . . ? [eel foh ahfrōn-sheer ah kōnb-yān poor]

» *TRAVEL TIP: you can buy stamps from many newsstands and some cafés; look for the sign "tabacs-journaux" or "tabac"*

stand *(at fair)* un stand [stōn]

standard normal

star une étoile [ay-twahl]

starboard: to starboard à tribord [ah tree-bor]

start commencer [kohmōn-say]

my car won't start ma voiture ne démarre pas [mah vwah-toor ner day-mar pah]

when does it start? ça commence quand? [sah koh-mōns kōn]

starter *(car)* le démarreur [daymah-rerr]

(dish) une entrée [ōn-tray]

starving: I'm starving je meurs de faim [jer merr der fān]

station la gare [gar]

(subway) la station de métro [stahs-yōn ...]

stationery store une papeterie [pahpet-ree]

stationnement parking

statue une statue [stah-too]

stay: we enjoyed our stay nous avons fait un très bon séjour [... say-joor]

stay there restez là [res-tay lah]

I'm staying at... je séjourne à ... [say-joorn]

can we stay here? est-ce que nous pouvons nous abriter ici? [... nooz ahbree-tay ee-see]

steak un steak [stek]

YOU MAY HEAR ...

à point [ah pwān] *medium*

bien cuit [bee-yān kwee] *well done*

saignant [sayn-yōn] *rare*

steal voler [voh-lay]

steep *(slope)* raide [red]

steering *(car)* la direction [deereks-yōn]

steering wheel le volant [voh-lōn]

step *(stairs)* une marche [marsh]

stereo stéréo [stay-ray-oh]

stewardess une hôtesse [oh-tes]

sticky poisseux [pwah-ser]

stiff dur [door]

still: keep still restez tranquille [res-tay trōn-keel]

I'm still here je suis encore là [jer swee ōn-kor ...]

stockings des bas [bah]

stolen: my wallet's been stolen on m'a volé mon portefeuille [ōn mah voh-lay ...]

stomach l'estomac [estoh-mah]

....

I've got a stomachache j'ai mal au ventre
[jay mal oh vōntr]
  **have you got something for an upset
stomach?** est-ce que vous avez quelque chose
pour les maux de ventre? [. . . moh der vōntr]
stone une pierre [pee-yair]
stop s'arrêter [. . . ahray-tay]
  do you stop near . . . ? est-ce que vous vous
arrêtez près de . . . ? [esker voo vooz ahray-tay
pray der]
  stop over une escale [es-kahl]
storm une tempête [tōn-pet]
stove la cuisinière [kweezee-nyair]
straight droit [drwah]
  (whisky, etc.) sec
  go straight ahead continuez tout droit
[kōntee-noo-ay too drwah]
strange bizarre
stranger un inconnu [āŋkoh-noo]
  I'm a stranger here je ne suis pas d'ici [jer
ner swee pah dee-see]
strap une courroie [koo-rwah]
strawberries des fraises [frayz]
street une rue [roo]
  a street map of un plan de [plōn]
strike une grève [graiv]
string de la ficelle [fee-sel]
stroke: he's had a stroke il a eu une attaque
[. . . ah-tak]
stroller une poussette [poo-set]
strong fort [for]
stuck coincé [kwāŋ-say]
student un étudiant [aytood-yōn]
stung: I've been stung by . . . j'ai été piqué
par . . . [jay ay-tay pee-kay par]
stupid stupide [stoo-peed]
suburbs la banlieue [bōnl-yer]
subway *(rail)* le métro [may-troh] *see* **métro**
successful: was it successful? est-ce que ça a
réussi? [esker sah ah ray-oo-see]
such: such a lot of . . . tant de . . . [tōn der]

suddenly subitement [soobeet-mōn]

suffer: he's suffering from il souffre de [soofr der]

sugar du sucre [sookr]

» TRAVEL TIP: *sugar in lumps is the rule; if you want granulated sugar, ask for "du sucre en poudre" [sookr ōn poodr]*

suit *(man's)* un complet [kōn-play]
(woman's) un tailleur [tay-yerr]

suitable: it's not suitable ça ne convient pas [sah ner kōnv-yān pah]

suitcase une valise [vah-leez]

summer l'été [ay-tay]

sun le soleil [soh-lay]
  in the sun au soleil
  out of the sun à l'abri du soleil [ah lah-bree . . .]
  sunbathe se bronzer [ser brōn-zay]
  sunburn un coup de soleil [koo . . .]
  sunglasses des lunettes de soleil [loo-net . . .]
  sunstroke une insolation [ānsoh-lahs-yōn]
  suntan oil de l'huile solaire [weel soh-lair]

Sunday dimanche [dee-mōnsh]

supermarket un supermarché [soopair-mar-shay]

» TRAVEL TIP: *often open on Sun. mornings*

sure: I'm not sure je ne suis pas sûr [. . . soor]
  sure! bien entendu! [bee-yānn ōntōn-doo]
  are you sure? vous êtes sûr? [vooz ayt soor]

surfboard une planche de surf [plōnsh der soorf]

surfing: to go surfing faire du surf [fair du soorf]

surname le nom de famille [nōn der fah-mee]

suspenders les bretelles [brer-tel]

sweat transpirer [trōnspee-ray]

sweater un pull [pool]

sweet: it's too sweet c'est trop sucré [. . . soo-kray]

swerve: I had to swerve j'ai dû donner un coup de volant [jay doo doh-nay ān koo der voh-lōn]

swim: I can't swim je ne sais pas nager [jer ner say pah nah-jay]

I'm going for a swim je vais me baigner [jer vay mer bayn-yay]

swimsuit un maillot de bain [mah-yoh der bān]

swimming trunks un slip de bain

swimming pool une piscine [pee-seen]

switch un interrupteur [āntay-roop-terr]

switch the light on/off allumez/éteignez la lumière [ahloo-may, aytayn-yay . . .]

switchboard le standard [stōn-dar]

Swiss suisse [swees]

Switzerland la Suisse [swees]

tabac-journaux *tobacconist and newsstand*

table: a table for 4 une table pour quatre [oon tahbl poor kahtr]

table wine du vin ordinaire [vān ohrdee-nair]

taille *size*

take prendre [prōndr]

can I take this with me? est-ce que je peux emporter ça? [. . . ōnpohr-tay]

take me to the airport emmenez-moi à l'aéroport [ōnm-nay mwah . . .]

can I take you out tonight? est-ce que vous voulez sortir avec moi ce soir? [. . . sohr-teer ah-vek mwah ser swahr]

is this seat taken? est-ce que cette place est prise? [. . . set plahs ay preez]

talcum powder du talc

talk parler [par-lay]

tall grand [grōn]

tampons des tampons hygiéniques [tōnpōn eej-yay-neek]

tan le bronzage [brōn-zahj]

I want to get a tan je veux bronzer [jer ver brōn-zay]

tank le réservoir [rayzair-vwahr]

tape une bande magnétique [bōnd mahn-yay-teek]

tape-recorder un magnétophone [mahn-yay-toh-fon]

tariff le tarif [tah-reef]

....

taste: what does it taste like? quel goût ça a?
  [kel goo sah ah]
  can I taste it? est-ce que je peux goûter?
  [esker jer per goo-tay]
  it tastes horrible/very nice c'est
  affreux/délicieux [sayt ah-frer, daylees-yer]
taxi un taxi [tah-xee]
  will you get me a taxi? est-ce que vous
  pouvez m'appeler un taxi? [. . . map-lay ān
  tah-xee]
  where can I get a taxi? où est-ce que je peux
  trouver un taxi?
  stop here arrêtez-vous ici [ahray-tay-voo
  ee-see]
  YOU MAY SEE . . .
  tête de station *taxi stand*
» *TRAVEL TIP: don't forget to tip (about 10%)*
T.C.F. = *Touring Club de France, similar to AAA*
tea le thé [tay]
  could I have a cup of tea? est-ce que je peux
  avoir un thé?
  a pot of tea for 2 une théière pour deux
  [tay-yair poor der]
  YOU MAY THEN HEAR . . .
  un thé lait [tay lay] *tea with milk*
  un thé citron [tay see-trōn] *tea with lemon*
» *TRAVEL TIP: tea is not automatically served with
  milk*
teach: could you teach me French? est-ce que
  vous pouvez m'apprendre le français?
  [. . . mah-prōndr ler frōn-say]
teacher le professeur [prohfay-serr]
teinturerie dry cleaner
telegram: I want to send a telegram je veux
  envoyer un télégramme [. . . ōnvwah-yay ān
  taylay-gram]
telephone le téléphone [taylay-fon]
  (where) can I make a phone call? (où) est-ce
  que je peux téléphoner? [. . . taylay-foh-nay]
  can I speak to . . . ? est-ce que je peux parler
  à . . . ? [esker jer per pahr-lay ah]

could you get this number for me? est-ce
que vous pouvez m'appeler ce numéro?
[. . . map-lay ser noomay-roh]
extension . . . poste numéro . . . [pohst
noomay-roh]
telephone booth une cabine téléphonique
[kah-been taylay-foh-neek]
telephone directory l'annuaire du téléphone
[ahnoo-air . . .]
YOU MAY HEAR . . .
qui est à l'appareil? *who's speaking?*
c'est un faux numéro *sorry wrong number*
la ligne est occupée *the line is busy*
ça ne répond pas *there is no answer*
ne quittez pas, je vous passe . . . *hold the line,
I'm putting you through to . . .*
» *TRAVEL TIP: you can phone from most cafés; pay
at counter or you may have to buy a "jeton"*
[jer-tōn] *(token) which you insert in the pay
phone; there are now more phone booths, esp.
in Paris (gray color): insert coin (50 centimes
for local call) before lifting receiver.*
television: I'd like to watch television
j'aimerais regarder la télévision [jaim-ray
rergahr-day lah taylay-veez-yōn]
tell: could you tell me where/if . . . ? est-ce que
vous pouvez me dire où/si . . . ? [esker voo poovay mer deer oo, see]
temperature la température [tōnpay-rah-toor]
temporary provisoire [prohvee-zwahr]
tennis: do you play tennis? est-ce que vous
jouez au tennis? [. . . joo-ay oh tay-nees]
tennis court un court de tennis [koor . . .]
tennis racquet une raquette de tennis
[rah-ket . . .]
tennis ball une balle de tennis [bahl . . .]
tent une tente [tōnt]
terminal le terminus [tairmee-noos]
terrible terrible [tay-reebl]
(bad) affreux [ah-frer]
terrific fantastique [fōntahs-teek]

than: bigger than... plus grand que...
[...ker]
thanks merci [mair-see]; **no thanks** non merci
thank you very much merci beaucoup
[...boh-koo]
thank you for your help merci de votre aide
that ce (cette) [ser, set]
that man/plane cet homme/avion [set...]
I would like that one j'aimerais celui-là
(celle-là) [...serlwee-lah, sel-lah]
and that? et ça? [...sah]
I think that... je crois que... [...ker]
the le (la), les [ler, lah, lay]
the children les enfants [layz...]
the airport l'aéroport
theater le théâtre [tay-ahtr]
their leur, leurs [lerr]
their car leur voiture, **their children** leurs
enfants
it's their suitcase, it's theirs c'est leur valise,
c'est la leur
them: with them avec eux (elles) [...er, al]
we didn't see them nous ne les avons pas vus
[...lay...]
we gave them the money nous leur avons
donné l'argent [...lerr...]
then ensuite [ōn-sweet]
there là [lah]
how do I get there? comment est-ce qu'on y
va? [koh-mōn eskōnn ee vah]
there is, there are il y a [eel-yah]
there isn't, there aren't il n'y a pas de [eeln-
yah pah der]
is there a bus? est-ce qu'il y a un bus?
[eskeel-yah...]
there you are (giving something) voilà
[vwah-lah]
thermos un thermos [tair-mohs]
these: these apples ces pommes [say...]
can I take these? est-ce que je peux prendre
ceux-ci (celles-ci)? [...ser-see, sel-see]

they ils (elles) [eel, el]
thick épais [ay-pay]
thief un voleur [voh-ler]
thigh la cuisse [kwees]
thin mince [mãns]
thing une chose [shohz]
   I've lost all my things j'ai perdu toutes mes affaires [jay pair-doo toot mayz ah-fair]
think: I'll think it over je vais y réfléchir [jer vayz ee rayflay-sheer]
   I think so je crois [jer krwah]
   I don't think so je ne crois pas
   I think that... je crois que...
third troisième [trwah-zem]
thirsty: I'm thirsty j'ai soif [jay swahf]
this ce (cette) [ser, set]
   this man/plane cet homme/avion [set...]
   I would like this one j'aimerais celui-ci (celle-ci) [serlwee-see, sel-see]
   this is my wife/Mr.... voici ma femme/Monsieur... [vwah-see...]
   this is... c'est... [say]
   is this...? est-ce que c'est...? [esker say]
   and this? et ça [...sah]
those: those people ces gens [say jõn]
   how much are those? combien coûtent ceux-ci (celles-ci)? [...ser-see, sel-see]
thread du fil [feel]
three trois [trwah]
throat la gorge [gorj]
   throat lozenges des pastilles pour la gorge [pas-tee...]
through à travers [ah trah-vair]
throw lancer [lõn-say]
thumb le pouce [poos]
   thumbtack une punaise [poo-nayz]
thunder le tonnerre [toh-nair]
   thunderstorm un orage [oh-rahj]
Thursday jeudi [jer-dee]
ticket un billet [bee-yay]
   ticket office le guichet [ghee-shay]

....

tie *(necktie)* une cravate [krah-vat]
tight *(clothes):* **they're too tight** ils sont trop
  justes [. . . joost]
time: what time is it? quelle heure il est? [kayl
  err eel ay]
  at what time? à quelle heure?
  I haven't got time je n'ai pas le temps [. . . ler
  tōn]
  for the time being pour le moment
  [. . . moh-mōn]
  this time cette fois [set fwah]
  last/next time la dernière/prochaine fois
  [dairn-yair, proh-shain fwah]
  3 times trois fois
  have a good time! amusez-vous bien!
  [ahmoo-zay-voo bee-yān]
  HOW TO TELL THE TIME:
  it's 2 a.m./p.m. c'est deux heures du matin/de
  l'après-midi [say derz err doo mahtān, der
  lah-pray-mee-dee]
  at 7 p.m. à sept heures du soir [ah set err doo
  swahr]
  2:05 deux heures cinq
  2:15 deux heures et quart [. . . ay kar]
  2:30 deux heures et demie [. . . ay der-mee]
  2:40 trois heures moins vingt [. . . mwān vān]
  2:45 trois heures moins le quart [. . . mwān ler
  kar]
timetable un horaire [oh-rair]
tip: is the tip included? est-ce que le pourboire
  est compris? [. . . poor-bwahr . . .]
» *TRAVEL TIP: tip ushers (about 2F), taxi drivers,*
  and restroom attendants (about 50 centimes)
tired: I'm tired je suis fatigué [fahtee-gay]
tirez pull
tissues des Kleenex
to: to Paris à Paris
  to our friends' chez [shay] nos amis
  to America en [ōn] Amérique
toast un toast [tohst]
tobacco du tabac [tah-bah]

tobacco store un bureau de tabac [boo-roh der tah-bah]

today aujourd'hui [ohjoor-dwee]

toe le doigt de pied [dwah der pee-yay]

together: we're together nous sommes ensemble [. . . o͞n-so͞nbl]

toilet: where are the toilets? où sont les toilettes? [oo so͞n lay twah-let]

 I have to go to the toilet je dois aller aux toilettes [jer dwahz ah-lay oh . . .]

 there's no toilet paper il n'y a pas de papier hygiénique [. . . pahp-yay eej-yay-neek]

 the ladies' room les toilettes (des dames) [twah-let day dam]

 the men's room les toilettes (des hommes)

 public rest rooms des toilettes [twah-let] publiques

» *TRAVEL TIP: public toilets are sometimes scarce and difficult to find; remember that cafés and bars always provide such facilities*

tomato une tomate [toh-mat]

 tomato juice un jus [joo] de tomate

tomorrow demain [der-ma͞n]

 tomorrow morning/afternoon/evening demain matin/après-midi/soir [der-ma͞n mah-ta͞n, ahpray-mee-dee, swahr]

 the day after tomorrow après-demain [ahpray-der-ma͞n]

ton une tonne [ton]

» *TRAVEL TIP: 1 ton = 1,016 kilos*

tongue la langue [lo͞ng]

tonic *(water)* un schweppes [shveps]

tonight ce soir [ser swahr]

tonsillitis une angine [o͞n-jeen]

tonsils les amygdales [ahmee-dahl]

too trop [troh]

 that's too much c'est trop

 too much . . . , too many . . . trop de . . .

tool un outil [oo-tee]

tooth une dent [do͞n]

....

I've got a toothache j'ai mal aux dents [jay mal oh dōn]
  toothbrush une brosse à dents [brohs ah dōn]
  toothpaste du dentifrice [dōntee-frees]
top: on top of sur [soor]
  on the top floor au dernier étage [oh dairn-yair ay-tahj]
  at the top en haut [ōn oh]
total le total [toh-tal]
tough dur [door]
tour une excursion [exkoors-yōn]
  we'd like to go on a tour of... nous aimerions visiter... [noozaymer-yōn veezee-tay]
  package tour un voyage organisé [voh-yahj orgah-nee-zay]
tourist: I'm a tourist je suis un touriste [... too-reest]
  tourist office le syndicat d'initiative [sāndee-kah deenees-yah-teev]
toutes directions through traffic
tow: can you give me a tow? est-ce que vous pouvez me remorquer? [... mer rermohr-kay]
  towrope une corde de dépannage [kord der daypah-nahj]
towards: he was coming straight towards me il venait droit vers moi [... drwah vair mwah]
towel une serviette [sairv-yet]
town une ville [veel]
  in town en ville
  would you take me into the town? est-ce que vous pouvez m'emmener en ville?
traditional traditionnel [trahdees-yoh-nel]
traffic la circulation [seerkoo-lahs-yōn]
  traffic lights les feux [fer]
  traffic policeman un agent de la circulation [ah-jōn...]
trailer une caravane [kahrah-van]
  trailer site un camping pour caravanes

train un train [trān]

» *TRAVEL TIP: you may have to punch your ticket before boarding the train; look for orange-colored machines located on platforms or for the notice "compostez votre billet"; children under 10 pay half-fare, go free under 4; there are extra charges on some inter-city trains*

traiteur delicatessen, caterers

tranquilizers des tranquillisants [trōnkee-lee-zōn]

translate: would you translate that for me? est-ce que vous pouvez me traduire ça? [. . . mer trah-dweer sah]

transmission *(of car)* la transmission [trōnsmees-yōn]

travaux road construction

travel: we're traveling around nous visitons la région [noo veezee-tōn la rayj-yōn]

travel agency une agence de voyage [ah-jōns der voh-yahj]

traveler's check un traveller's cheque

tree un arbre [ahrbr]

trip un voyage [voh-yahj]

(short tour, drive) une excusion [exkoors-yōn]

we want to go on a trip to . . . nous voulons faire une excusion à . . .

trouble: I'm having trouble with . . . j'ai des ennuis avec . . . [jay dayz ōnn-wee ah-vek]

trousers un pantalon [pōntah-lōn]

truck un camion [kahm-yōn]

truck driver un chauffeur de camion [shoh-ferr . . .]

true vrai [vray]

trunk *(of car)* le coffre [kofr]

trunks *(swimming)* un slip de bain [. . . der bān]

try essayer [essay-yay]

can I try? est-ce que je peux essayer? [esker jer per aysay-yay]

can I try it on? est-ce que je peux l'essayer?

T-shirt un T-shirt

t.t.c. = *toutes taxes comprises (all taxes included)*

Tuesday mardi [mahr-dee]
tunnel un tunnel [too-nel]
turn: where do we turn off? où est-ce qu'il faut tourner? [wes-keel foh toor-nay]
  he turned without indicating il a tourné sans mettre le clignotant [. . . ler kleen-yoh-tōn]
  it's my turn c'est ma tournée [say mah toor-nay]
T.V.A. [tay-vay-ah] *sales tax*
twice deux fois [der fwah]
twin beds des lits jumeaux [lee joo-moh]
  twin room une chambre à deux lits [shōnbr ah der lee]
two deux [der]
typewriter une machine à écrire [mah-sheen ah ay-kreer]
typical typique [tee-peek]
tire un pneu [pner]
  I need a new tire il me faut un pneu neuf [eel mer foh ān pner nerf]
» *TRAVEL TIP: tire pressures*

lb/sq in	18	20	22	24	26	28	30
kg/sq cm	1.3	1.4	1.5	1.7	1.8	2	2.1

ugly laid [lay]
ulcer un ulcère [ool-sair]
  (in mouth) un aphte [ahft]
umbrella un parapluie [pahrah-plwee]
uncle: my uncle mon oncle [ōnkl]
uncomfortable inconfortable [ānkōn-for-tahbl]
unconscious: he is unconscious il a perdu connaissance [eel ah pair-doo kohnay-sōns]
under sous [soo]
  he's under 12 il a moins de douze ans [eel ah mwān der . . .]
underdone pas assez cuit [pahz ah-say kwee]
underexposed sous-exposé [soozex-poh-zay]
understand: I don't understand je ne comprends pas [jer ner kōn-prōn pah]
  do you understand? est-ce que vous comprenez? [. . . kōnprer-nay]

underwear *(shorts)* un slip
undo défaire [day-fair]
United States les Etats-Unis [aytahz-oo-nee]
university l'université [oonee-vair-see-tay]
unlock ouvrir [oo-vreer]
until jusqu'à [joos-kah]
    until July jusqu'en juillet [joos-k$\overline{on}$ ...]
unusual inhabituel [eenah-bee-too-el]
up en haut [$\overline{on}$ oh]
    he's not up yet il n'est pas encore levé [eel
nay pahz $\overline{on}$-kor ler-vay]
upside down à l'envers [ah l$\overline{on}$-vair]
upstairs en haut [$\overline{on}$ oh]
urgent urgent [oor-j$\overline{on}$]
us nous [noo]
USA les USA [oo-es-ah]
use: can I use ...? est-ce que je peux
utiliser ... ? [esker jer per ootee-lee-zay]
useful utile [oo-teel]
usual habituel [ahbee-too-el]
    as usual comme d'habitude [kom dahbee-tood]
    usually d'habitude [dahbee-tood]
U-turn un demi-tour [der-mee-toor]
vacancy: do you have any vacancies? est-ce
que vous avez de la place? [... der lah plahs]
vacate *(room)* libérer [leebay-ray]
vacation les vacances [vah-k$\overline{on}$s]
    I'm on vacation je suis en vacances [jer
sweez $\overline{on}$ ...]
vaccination un vaccin [vak-s$\overline{an}$]
valid: how long is it valid for? c'est valable
combien de temps? [say vah-lahbl k$\overline{on}$b-y$\overline{an}$
der t$\overline{on}$]
valley une vallée [vah-lay]
valuable: it's valuable ça a de la valeur
[... vah-lerr]
    will you look after my valuables? est-ce
que vous pouvez me garder mes objets de
valeur? [... mer gahr-day mayz ob-jay der
vah-lerr]
value la valeur [vah-lerr]

valves *(of car)* les soupapes [soo-pap]
van une camionnette [kahm-yoh-net]
vanilla *(ice-cream)* à la vanille [ah lah vah-nee]
varicose veins des varices [vah-rees]
veal du veau [voh]
vegetables des légumes [lay-goom]
vegetarian végétarien [vayjay-tahr-yān]
vendre: à vendre for sale
ventilator un ventilateur [vōntee-lah-terr]
very très [tray]
  very much beaucoup [boh-koo]
view la vue [voo]
via par
village un village [vee-lahj]
vine une vigne [veen]
vinegar du vinaigre [vee-naigr]
vineyard un vignoble [veen-yohbl]
vintage: a good vintage une bonne année [bon
  ah-nay]
violent violent [vee-yoh-lōn]
virages bends
visibility la visibilité [veezee-bee-lee-tay]
visit visiter [veezee-tay]
  visitor une visite [vee-zeet]
vitesse limitée à . . . speed limit. . .
voice la voix [vwah]
voie 6 platform 6
voltage le voltage [vol-tahj]
  is it 220V? est-ce que c'est du deux cent vingt
  volts? [. . . doo der sōn vān vohlt]
waist la taille [tie]
» *TRAVEL TIP: waist measurements*

US	24	26	28	30	32	34	36	38
Continent	61	66	71	76	80	87	91	97

wait: will we have to wait long? est-ce qu'il
  faudra attendre longtemps [eskeel foh-drah
  ah-tōndr lōn-tōn]
  wait for me! attendez-moi! [ahtōn-day-mwah]
  I'm waiting for j'attends [jah-tōn]
waiter le serveur [sair-verr]
  waiter! s'il vous plaît! [seel voo play]

waitress la serveuse [sair-verz]
   waitress! s'il vous plaît! [seel-voo play]
wake: will you wake me up at 7:30? est-ce que
   vous pouvez me réveiller à 7:30? [. . . mer
   rayvay-yay . . .]
Wales le Pays de Galles [payee der gal]
walk: can we walk there? est-ce qu'on peut y
   aller à pied? [. . . ee ah-lay ah pee-yay]
   are there any good walks around here?
   est-ce qu'il y a des promenades intéressantes
   dans les environs? [. . . day prohm-nad
   $\overline{\text{an}}$tay-ray-s$\overline{\text{on}}$t . . .]
   walking shoes des chaussures de marche
   [shoh-soor der marsh]
wall le mur [moor]
wallet un portefeuille [pohrter-fer-ee]
want: I want . . . je voudrais . . . [jer voo-dray]
   I want to talk to . . . je voudrais parler à . . .
   (note that you can say "je veux", but "je
   voudrais" is more courteous)
   we want . . . nous voulons . . . [noo voo-l$\overline{\text{on}}$]
   he wants . . . il veut . . . [eel ver]
   what do you want? qu'est-ce que vous voulez?
   [kesker voo voo-lay]
   I don't want . . . je ne veux pas . . . [jer ner
   ver pah]
war la guerre [gair]
warm chaud [shoh]
warn avertir [ahvair-teer]
wash: can you wash these for me? est-ce que
   vous pouvez me laver ça? [. . . mer lah-vay sah]
   where can I wash? où est-ce que je peux me
   laver? [wesker jer per mer lah-vay]
   washable lavable [lah-vahbl]
washer *(for faucet, etc.)* un joint [jw$\overline{\text{an}}$]
wasp une guêpe [gaip]
wastebasket une poubelle [poo-bel]
watch *(wrist-)* une montre [m$\overline{\text{on}}$tr]
   my watch is slow/fast ma montre
   retarde/avance [. . . rer-tahrd, ah-v$\overline{\text{on}}$s]

will you watch my bags for me? est-ce que vous pouvez surveiller mes bagages? [. . . soor-vay-yay may bah-gahj]

watch out! attention! [ahtōns-yon]

watch strap un bracelet de montre [brahs-lay]

water l'eau [oh]

can I have some water? est-ce que je peux avoir de l'eau?

hot and cold running water eau courante chaude et froide [oh koo-rōnt shohd ay frwad]

waterproof imperméable [ānpair-may-ahbl]

waterskiing le ski nautique [skee noh-teek]

way: the French way à la française [ah lah frōn-sayz]

could you tell me the way to . . . ? quel est le chemin pour aller à . . . ? [kel ay ler sher-mān poor ah-lay ah]

YOU MAY THEN HEAR . . .

tournez . . . , prenez . . . *turn* . . . , *go* . . .

à droite *right*, à gauche *left*

continuez tout droit *go straight*

aux feux *at the lights*

we nous [noo]

weak faible [faibl]

weather le temps [tōn]

what's the weather like in . . . ? quel temps est-ce qu'il fait à . . . [kel tōn eskeel fay ah]

what's the weather forecast? quelles sont les prévisions de la météo [. . . lay prayveez-yōn der lah maytay-oh]

YOU MAY THEN HEAR . . .

couvert *overcast,* du soleil *sunny,* de la neige *snow,* de la pluie *rain,* du vent *wind,* (très) froid *(very) cold,* (très) chaud *(very) warm*

wedding un mariage [mahr-yahj]

Wednesday mercredi [mairkrer-dee]

week une semaine [ser-men]

a week from today dans huit jours [dōn wee joor]

a week from tomorrow/on Monday
demain/lundi en huit [der-mān, lān-dee ōn
weet]

at the weekend le weekend [wee-kend]

weigh: can you weigh this for me? est-ce que
vous pouvez me peser ça? [. . . mer per-zay sah]

weight le poids [pwah]

well: I'm not feeling well je ne me sens pas très
bien [jer ner mer sōn pah tray bee-yān]

he's not well il ne va pas bien [eel ner vah
pah bee-yān]

very well thanks très bien, merci [tray
bee-yān mair-see]

Welsh gallois [gal-wah]

west l'ouest [oo-est]

West Indies les Antilles [ōn-tee]

wet mouillé [moo-yay]; *(weather)* humide
[oo-meed]

wet suit combinaison de plongée
[kōnbee-nay-zōn der plōn-jay]

wharf un quai [kay]

what quel (quelle) [kel]

what is that? qu'est-ce que c'est? [kesker say]

what for? pourquoi? [poor-kwah]

what's that in French? comment est-ce que
ça se dit en français? [koh-mōnt esker sah ser
dee ōn frōn-say]

wheel une roue [roo]

wheelchair un fauteuil roulant [foh-ter roo-lōn]

when quand [kōn]

when is breakfast? à quelle heure est le
petit déjeuner? [ah kel err . . .]

where où [oo]

where is . . . ? où est . . . ? [oo ay]

where is it? où est-ce que c'est? [wesker say]

where can we . . . ? où est-ce qu'on peut . . . ?

YOU MAY THEN HEAR . . .

près d'ici *nearby*

près de . . . *close to . . .*

très loin *very far*

which quel (quelle) [kel]

which one? lequel (laquelle)? [ler-kel, lah-kel]
YOU MAY THEN HEAR...
celui-ci *this one*, celui-là *that one*
whisky un whisky
white blanc [blon]
who qui [kee]
wholesale price le prix de gros [pree der groh]
whose: whose is this? à qui est ceci? [ah kee ...]
why pourquoi [poor-kwah]
why not? pourquoi pas?
YOU MAY HEAR...
parce que... *because...*
wide large [lahrj]
width la largeur [lahr-jerr]
wife: my wife ma femme [fam]
will: will you do it? est-ce que vous pouvez le
faire? [esker voo poo-vay ler fair]
I will come back je reviendrai [rerv-yan-dray]
NB: *here is the French future tense with the
verb "prendre": je prendrai, il prendra, nous
prendrons, vous prendrez, ils prendront; with
"parler": je parlerai, etc.*
win gagner [gahn-yay]
who won? qui a gagné? [kee ah gahn-yay]
wind le vent [von]
window le fenêtre [fer-naitr]
(of car) la vitre [veetr]
it's in the window c'est dans la vitrine [say
don lah vee-treen]
windshield le pare-brise [par-breez]
windshield wipers les essuie-glace [ay-swee
glahs]
windy: it's too windy il y a trop de vent [eelyah
troh der von]
wine du vin [van]
wine list la carte des vins [kart day van]
red wine du vin rouge [... rooj]
white wine du vin blanc [... blon]
» *TRAVEL TIP: enjoy the simpler "vins de table" or
"vins de pays", they are generally good quality
and cheap*

winter l'hiver [ee-vair]
wire du fil métallique [feel maytah-leek]
   (electrical) un fil électrique [. . . aylek-treek]
wish: best wishes meilleurs voeux [may-yerr ver]
   (on letter) meilleures pensées [. . . pōn-say]
with avec [ah-vek]
without sans [sōn]
witness un témoin [tay-mwān]
   will you be a witness for me? est-ce que
   vous pouvez me servir de témoin? [. . . mer
   sair-veer . . .]
woman une femme [fam]
wonderful magnifique [mahnee-feek]
wood du bois [bwah]
   (forest) un bois
wool de la laine [len]
word un mot [moh]
   I don't know what word je ne connais pas ce
   mot [jer ner koh-nay pah ser moh]
work travailler [travah-yay]
   it's not working ça ne marche pas [sah ner
   marsh pah]
   how does it work? comment ça marche?
   I work in New York je travaille à New York
   [jer trah-vie . . .]
worn out usé [oo-zay]
worry les soucis [soo-see]
   don't worry ne vous inquiétez pas [ner vooz
   ānk-yay-tay pah]
   I'm worried about . . . je suis inquiet
   pour . . . [jer swee ānk-yay poor]
worse: it's worse c'est pire [say peer]
   he's getting worse son état s'aggrave [sōn ay-
   tah sah-grahv]
   the worst le pire
worth: it's not worth that much ça ne vaut pas
   autant [sah ner voh pah oh-tōn]
   is it worthwhile going to . . . ? est-ce que ça
   vaut la peine d'aller à . . . ? [esker sah voh lah
   pen dah-lay ah]

50F worth of gas pour cinquante francs d'essence [poor . . .]

wrap: could you wrap it up? est-ce que vous pouvez me l'envelopper? [. . . mer lōnv-loh-pay]

wrench une clé anglaise [klay ōn-glayz]

wrist le poignet [pwahn-yay]

write écrire [ay-kreer]

　could you write it down? est-ce que vous pouvez me l'écrire?

　I'll write to you je vous écrirai [jer vooz aykree-ray]

　writing paper du papier à lettres [pahp-yay ah laitr]

wrong: I think the bill's wrong je crois qu'il y a une erreur dans l'addition [jer krwah keel yah oon ay-rerr dōn lahdees-yōn]

　there's something wrong with . . . il y a quelque chose qui ne va pas dans . . . [eelyah kelker-shoz kee ne vah pah dōn]

　sorry, wrong number! excusez-moi, j'ai fait un faux numéro [exkoo-zay mwah jay fay ān foh noomay-roh]

　you are wrong vous vous trompez [voo voo trōn-pay]

X-ray une radio [rahd-yoh]

yacht un yacht [yot]

yard

　» *TRAVEL TIP: 1 yard = 91.44 cm = 0.91 m*

year une année [ah-nay]

　this year cette année

　next year l'année prochaine [. . . proh-shain]

yellow jaune [jon]

yes oui [wee]

yesterday hier [yair]

　the day before yesterday avant-hier [ahvōnt-yair]

　yesterday morning/afternoon hier matin/après-midi [. . . mah-tān, ahpray-mee-dee]

yet: is it ready yet? est-ce que c'est déjà prêt? [esker say day-jah pray]